D0759111

A Home OF YOUr OWN

A Home of Your Own

Creating Interiors with Character

Sally Coulthard

MERRELL
LONDON · NEW YORK

Introduction

What do we mean when we say
someone's home has 'character'?
We use the word all the time,
but may be hard pressed to
pin down exactly what makes
a particular space special.

In a period house, an estate agent might point to the wealth of original features or pleasing proportions, but these qualities alone are not what gives a home character: there are plenty of fine historic houses that feel cold and unwelcoming. Equally, in a building with little or no architectural merit, one can find spaces packed with personality, humanity and joy. You have only to visit an artist's studio to see how a creative person can transform a dull, lifeless space.

When we describe a house as being characterful, what we mean is that it is individual, exceptional in some way; that the space has a special mix of features that, when put together, create a wonderfully idiosyncratic, interesting home. What's more, we are not referring simply to the building itself. The contents, colour scheme, layout and personal effects have just as much influence as, if not more than, structure in creating a unique, characterful home.

Uniqueness in our homes matters to us for many reasons. As human beings, we have an instinctive urge to mark our territory, to put our own stamp on our living space, to say: 'This is mine!' In addition, buildings have the power to evoke a response, as architects have long understood. These designers create spaces that are intended to communicate a message, to make us feel something. It is a 'language' we all speak and understand, even if we don't realize it.

As individuals, we too use this language in our own homes, endlessly creating, reworking and maintaining our nests. We do this because we want our homes to reflect

Page 7
In this Georgian-inspired panelled living room, reclaimed timber, second-hand furniture and family pieces full of history and meaning were used to create character from scratch.

Left
Homes don't have to be old to be characterful. This mid-twentieth-century artist's pad sparkles with personality, thanks to such treasured finds as vintage mirrors and flea-market chairs.

Opposite, top
Even functional spaces can reflect their occupants' personality. The owner of this galley kitchen has proudly displayed his collection of 1950s and 1960s kitchenalia and crockery.

Opposite, bottom
Paintings, heirlooms and favourite ornaments reflect our family life and friendships, as well as our interests and achievements.

who we are, as well as fulfil our basic need for shelter. Every time we choose a paint colour, hang a picture or pick out a fabric, we are communicating something to ourselves and to others. When we display a collection of teacups or trophies, we are letting people know our interests, values, ideals, tastes and preoccupations. And when we stack books on shelves or frame photographs, we are designing our homes to reflect our learning, our experiences and our relationships. Surrounding ourselves with our favourite objects helps us to affirm our identity.

A characterful home should therefore speak to us about the people who live in it.

The owner of this collection of paintings, glass paperweights, mirrors and other ornaments has become curator of his own home, frequently adding to and editing an exciting display.

Above
A personal twist can transform traditional notions, as in this quirky assortment of classical artefacts.

Homely style and handcrafted objects, such as this heirloom quilt, radiate character and charm, adding humanity and warmth to any living space.

When we step into one of our rooms, we want it to echo what's important to us, to say something about our past and our aspirations. We also want our home to reveal what we value about our family life, our passions and our pastimes.

Character in a home comes from a variety of sources: from the building itself, from the decoration and from the personalities of the people who live there. Only by unpicking these elements can we hope to understand their power. This book takes a closer look at the key ingredients that contribute to creating a characterful home. Individual chapters focus on the value of period features, and of antique, vintage and retro furnishings; on how to create living spaces that remind us of family, friends and loved ones; on the importance of expressing human creativity; on how to bring the outside in through natural materials and other reflections of outdoor life; on embracing craftsmanship and quality; and on how to include humour and playfulness. Throughout the book, 'Keys to Character' features, marked by an icon of a key, offer tips on incorporating personality, from creating quirky corners, via mixing and matching vintage pieces, to making the most of family heirlooms and photographs. The book concludes with an

If your home has period features, show them off. This building's inherent attributes, such as well-worn floorboards and a welcoming hob grate, add a rich layer of character.

Below
A home needs to feel lived in.
This kitchen, stuffed with a
lifetime's worth of teapots,
cups and country ornaments,
is a well-used, much-loved
hub where busy family life
is played out.

Opposite
Convivial spaces are the heart
of a characterful home. Here,
an old armchair sits next to
a glowing range to create a
cosy corner.

invaluable international directory of sources of information and of suppliers.

You don't necessarily need all the above-mentioned ingredients in equal amounts to create a space that is packed with personality; as you'll discover in these pages, the human elements are the most important. That doesn't mean the building has no impact, however. You can create character in a newly built property, but, if you're lucky enough to live in an older house, the quirks and charm of the building can, and should, add significantly to the mix.

If a building has no inherent character (which is actually rarer than one might think, since few things made by people are devoid of character), you'll have to compensate by adding more of your own. If your house has bags of character when you move in, a relationship between you and the building will have to be negotiated in order to get the best results. It's rather as with a marriage: both parties need to express themselves. Suppress either personality – and buildings do have personalities – and the result will be a deeply unsettling space. Period houses

that have had their original layouts and features ripped out, covered up or altered beyond all recognition cease to feel 'right'. Equally, an old building that has been meticulously and sensitively restored, but lacks any of the owner's possessions and personal touches, will only ever feel like a museum.

There are a number of reasons why a home might lack character. For a start, it may be *too* perfect, and feel as if no one lives there. There may be no evidence of people eating, sleeping, enjoying themselves; everything may be too clean, too new, too stark. Minimalist homes can sometimes suffer from this. Alternatively, a home may feel bland because it is too uniform: all the furniture and contents match, but in a way that leaves the space looking like a showroom in which everything is over-coordinated.

More importantly, a home will lack character because it contains nothing unique to the person who lives in it: no photographs, no personal treasures, no sign of pastimes or passions. Any pictures on the wall are there to fill a void, to break up the deafening silence of blank space. The person who lives here has invested no energy into personalizing his or her living space. It's the rental-property syndrome.

Homes with character hit you as soon as you walk through the door. They are visually appealing places, but more than that, they exude warmth, laughter and love. They reflect and bolster the ideals of the people who live in them. They celebrate the good things in life – family, friendship and human expression. They express pride

Opposite, top
A home's personality can be felt at the front door. Here, a stark whitewash and contrasting highlights make the hallway come alive.

Opposite, bottom
Characterful collections are never over-harmonized. This selection of white sculpture, ceramics and other trinkets is brought into relief with a bright splash of colour.

Right
This spare, rustic interior scheme gives the room's period features and furnishings a chance to shine, showing that there can be character in simplicity.

Opposite
Aubergine panelling shows
that colour and character
go hand in hand, helping to
engender a specific mood, draw
out architectural features and
provide a rich backdrop for
personal possessions.

Right
Mixing old and new, rustic and
contemporary, is a sure-fire
recipe for an exciting, eclectic
interior. Here, a simple white
limewash on the walls provides
the perfect canvas for folk art
and a striking modern chair.

in workmanship, art and creative endeavour.
They commemorate the fact that life is a
journey, full of treasured moments and
special occasions to be remembered. They
accept and proudly display all the bumps
and knocks that come with a life lived to the
full. Above all, they celebrate all that is great
about being human.

We all want to connect with our living
space, to create a home that not only
celebrates the past but also embraces our
personality; to make a space that helps to
remind us about all the things that matter to
us, whatever they are. That's real character.

Bold pieces of furniture, such as
this sturdy settle, and unusual,
naïve accessories create a witty
yet relaxed living space full of
drama and narrative.

Bumps, Bangs and Scratches

Character and history are natural bedfellows, yet the link between them isn't as straightforward as we might imagine. When we say that an old house has 'character', we may be admiring the fireplace or the original cornicing, but period features on their own cannot create character. Rather, through these attributes the building is talking to us about its past, revealing glimpses of its previous incarnations through its creaky wooden stairs, sturdy doors and antique tiles. Every worn floorboard speaks of thousands of footsteps.

To bring character to a building, we need to add our own story, in the form of salvage, antiques, vintage or retro pieces, heirlooms or simply objects from our lives that mean something to us. Surrounding ourselves with nostalgia and history helps us to plug into the past, making us feel grounded in the present and confident about looking to the future.

Whether in a cottage full of period features (above), an apartment of retro chic (above, right) or a bedroom decked out in vintage decor (right), a sense of the past helps us to feel rooted in the here and now.

Letting
Your Home
Tell a Story

Period features in a home tell us much about everyday life before we moved into it, how people would have lived, laughed and loved. As we warm ourselves gratefully in front of an open fire or bathe in a glorious cast-iron tub, it's not difficult to imagine previous occupants doing the same. This is pleasing to us, because we crave to feel connected to our past. Old houses thrill us because they provide an instant, physical way of reaching into our ancestry. Rather than making us feel insignificant in the grand scheme of things, this connection to the past in fact makes us feel more secure. An old property can be reassuringly solid, reliable and timeless, however insecure life might feel at times.

Left, top
Dark woods and a heavy wallpaper add to the ageless appeal of this masculine room. An original fireplace injects emotional warmth.

Left
The natural imperfections and gentle variations in old bricks make a pleasingly contrasting backdrop for crisp white bedding and refined antiques.

Old limed floorboards and a period staircase blend beautifully with the painted furniture and pale collectibles in this muted, Scandinavian-inspired home.

One of the main criticisms levelled at new houses is that they are very similar and feel bland. We enjoy the distinctiveness that comes from period features. However alike the houses in a Victorian terrace when they were first built, after a century of use each property will be unique. Decades of family life, refurbishment work and weathering will have given each house its own personality and rhythm.

But even in the newest of homes, there are many ways in which a sense of history and permanence can be generated, including using reclaimed materials and introducing vintage fixtures and furnishings. Making a characterful home is all about acknowledging and enjoying the passage of time.

Left, top
Years of family life and decor changes turn every old house into a unique living space, as this Victorian hallway demonstrates with its idiosyncratic curios.

Far left
The companionable crackle of an open fire is a timeless pleasure that will have been enjoyed by the generations who have passed through this Victorian home.

Left
This cosy attic shows that there is nothing to match the honest construction and quirky room shapes that come with vernacular building materials and traditional building techniques.

Celebrating Period Features

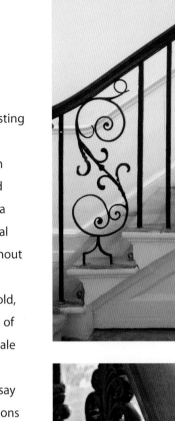

If you are lucky enough to live in an old house, an instant way to bring out its character is to make the most of any existing period features, such as fireplaces, floorboards, stained glass and bathroom fittings. These architectural gems should be cherished, as not only do they relate a story but also they are part of the original concept and design of the building; without them, a period home feels incomplete, unfinished. If your house is particularly old, the features may belong to a succession of periods and styles, each telling its own tale about the history of the house and the whims of its occupants. Period features say much about the ideals, wealth and fashions of times gone by, and they are a fascinating social record as well as allowing a glimpse into the aesthetics of the past.

There are dozens of books dedicated to the art of restoring period features, and if you are planning to bring an old house back to life then it pays to do your research. While this chapter can only skim over the topic and highlight the reasons why these features matter in the pursuit of character, the crucial point to make is that you should try not to be too selective about what you preserve. Original fireplaces and beams are usually retained by homeowners, but many other period features can get lost in the process of renovation and redecoration.

Right, top
Ornate iron balusters transform an everyday set of stairs into an exquisite architectural feature, one that is central to the balance and aesthetic of this period building.

Right
A voluted or monkey-tail handrail. The staircase is one of the key defining features of an old house, and yet it is often the first thing to be ripped out in unsympathetic conversions.

A period property's floorboards, cornicing, tiles, skirting boards, architraves, staircases, windows, stained glass, cupboards, screens, shutters and bathroom suites: all these elements should shine through if you are lucky enough to have them. More 'modern' period fittings are also starting to attract the attention of careful house restorers; fixtures from any decade up to the 1950s are worth preserving, especially if they're right for the period in which the building was constructed. Look out for original linoleum floors, Bakelite light switches, aluminium kitchen units, tiled fireplaces and unusual windows, including steel Crittall frames and sunburst designs.

Also significant are such period details as doorknobs, locks, window catches and taps. Each of these tiny historical elements contributes to the overall impact of a room. Other ephemeral or workaday details are precious, too. Rare survivors, such as scraps of ancient wallpaper, old lime plasterwork or an old painted cupboard interior, will sparkle if given room to breathe or highlighted in some way.

Left and above
Exposed timbers and roof beams provide visual texture and interest, but also give us a fascinating glimpse into the handcrafted building methods of our ancestors.

Variety of design and quality of workmanship in even the smallest details are beautifully demonstrated in this assortment of antique door handles and locks.

The Well-worn Interior

The most successful restorations are those that use a light touch on period features. When it comes to killing character, over-restoration is as destructive as leaving a house to fall into disrepair. Enthusiastic house renovators who end up disappointed with the results of their labours will often find that they have unwittingly removed most of the charm and softness that first drew them to the property.

There's a fine line between returning something to its former glory and making it look too new. Resist the temptation to peel back every layer of paint and patina; these are the surfaces and textures that give a home its charm. Don't worry if a surface is scratched, peeling, marked or crackly.

Opposite
An elegant vintage bathtub and washstand turn the mundane routine of washing into an enchanting, timeless pleasure.

Left and above
Well-worn surfaces, such as those of a battered door or a rustic kitchen table, have visual and tactile appeal and are proof of years of use.

Battered floors, flaking paint, well-worn stone: there's beauty and poignancy in materials that have been submitted to years of human use. It's all part of the appeal, and it's the reason why so many people pay for furniture and fittings that have been artificially aged. But rarely can fake compare to the genuine article. If we can resist the urge to rid every surface of cracks, bumps and scratches, and instead embrace the wear and tear of time, a period home will look and feel better for it.

If a surface needs cleaning or mending, use a light hand. Gentle, traditional finishes, such as beeswax, limewash, linseed oil, dead flat emulsion paint and black lead polish, will protect and repair more sensitively than modern polyurethane varnishes or vinyl paints. In recent years the market for conservation and heritage products has developed dramatically, so it's not difficult to find mainstream DIY stores selling products made with traditional, natural or eco-friendly formulas.

When cleaning an object's rough surfaces, scuffs and marks, try to preserve as much of the original patina as you can or you could end up removing everything that drew you to the piece in the first place.

The Joy of Reclamation

The careful use of reclaimed materials and architectural antiques, such as fireplaces and floorboards, can restore a ravaged period building to its former glory.

If your home has had its period features ripped out or you want to add warmth to a newly built property, architectural salvage can create character in an instant. Unlike modern reproductions, reclaimed period details will be made from building materials that fit the period style of your home, and will be of a quality unmatched by modern standards. Period features tend to have been fabricated from materials that are now unavailable or in short supply, such as mahogany, marble or pitch pine, so it's a real treat to incorporate these into your home. They're also a fraction of the price of a modern copy, and you can pat yourself on the back for recycling something that might otherwise have ended up in a skip.

Salvage can be used in two ways, both of which will add character and personality to the home. The first is to reinstate something that would have been there originally. Dedicated house restorers can spend many happy weekends trawling through reclamation yards to find a missing period door or a pallet of handmade bricks so as to complete a sensitive restoration. It's the ultimate treasure hunt, and nothing beats the satisfaction of fitting an old fireplace or door back where it belongs. You also know you've done the right thing when you cease to notice the feature. As with good dentistry or a fantastic restoration of a painting, the

best pieces of salvage are those that blend in seamlessly.

If you own a modern home, or have a more quirky approach to aesthetics, the second way of using salvage is as a fantastic opportunity for creative design. In some of the most interesting, eye-catching homes, architectural antiques have been used in exciting, obscure or even subversive ways. Pieces of salvage are historic survivors, one-offs, so no two interiors featuring reclaimed items can ever be the same. And that's the appeal: you can create a space that is as individual and adventurous as you are.

Salvage comes from an almost infinite variety of sources, so it gives great scope for originality. Such treasures as commercial neon signs, chapel lecterns, Victorian toilets and old film sets can inject real mischief into an interior if you play around with traditional notions of what should go where. A later chapter will delve further into the importance of visual surprises and humour in a characterful home (see pp. 152–81), but suffice it to say here that salvage is one of the easiest, quickest ways to achieve them.

Reclaimed and patinated wooden surfaces sit well together, regardless of age. Here, the screen, table and floorboards are unified against a neutral background.

The drawing out of similarities in colour and material has achieved an elegant harmonization of naïve folk furniture with an ornate rococo armchair, rustic accessories and bare plaster.

The Appeal of Antiques, Vintage and Retro

Period features and architectural details may be the bones of a characterful house, but you can introduce history and a sense of continuity through furniture and accessories, too. Furnishing your home with antiques – whether Regency sideboards or rustic kitchenalia – adds depth and vitality, a new layer of character and interest.

A quick dip into the history books brings an interesting insight: that collecting and displaying old 'stuff' is as ancient as civilization itself. When in the early 1920s the English Egyptologist Howard Carter opened the tomb of the fourteenth-century-BC pharaoh Tutankhamun, it contained a 'dynastic museum' of objects from different periods and countries. It seems the pharaoh had a keen eye for antiques. He wasn't the only one. In the third century BC Greek homeowners were already looking back to older styles and fashions, to the extent that Athenian workshops were producing reproductions and copies of earlier works.

Two plywood DCM chairs designed in the mid-twentieth century by Charles and Ray Eames add balance and symmetry to a wall of modern art, showing that retro furniture can be as elegant and sophisticated as even the most prized antique pieces.

A touch of 1930s glamour lifts this little corner into a different league. An art deco cabinet jostles for attention with vintage luggage, retro lighting and a Bakelite telephone.

People have antiques in their homes for many reasons. These older objects open a window into a different world, allowing us a tangible sense of a period in which techniques and tastes were different. Antiques speak of a 'golden age', of a time that, to some, seems more appealing than the modern world. We may collect them to show off our knowledge or connoisseurship of a particular maker or trend. Or perhaps the aesthetic of a specific period appeals to us more than the fashions of today; many eras have distinctive motifs and patterns, from the slender, spare elegance of the late Georgian period to the sinuous curves of art nouveau. Adding well-chosen, personal antiques to an interior scheme says something very specific about a person's tastes and priorities, about his or her views on what is important and beautiful in the world. In contrast, a flat-pack bookcase from a local superstore may be practical, but it says nothing about the people who put it together.

For many of us, however, antiques have been acquired or inherited over the years, often without our express choosing. We live with them because we feel we should keep them or because they remind us of a special person. Every knock and bump speaks of an event or a memory. We remember the Victorian coffee table sitting in the corner of our grandmother's house, piled high with afternoon tea, or a favourite aunt snoozing after Christmas lunch in her battered Edwardian armchair. Inherited antiques are often the only reminder we have of relatives either distant or deceased. Whether they

Left
The sweeping lines and stark beauty of this vintage chair are ageless, allowing it to fit either a highly contemporary or a very traditional interior.

The appeal of vintage and retro furniture, such as this 'space age' dining set, often lies in the fact that they connect us to our own past.

A retro chair – an all-wood version of the Eames DCM chair shown on p. 32 – and a lofty lamp have a striking presence against a simple mirror and minimalist backdrop.

Above, left
Many of us inherit a mishmash of pieces over the years. This dynamic collection of furniture and garden ornaments demonstrates that old pieces can be incorporated into the home in new and exciting ways to create a very personal style.

Above
A 1960s sky-blue armchair lifts this Victorian interior, adding visual zing and a welcome change in aesthetic from the heavy fireplace and shutters.

In this successful mixing up of eras, a nineteenth-century roll-top bath is teamed with a contemporary swivel chair by the French designer Philippe Starck and vintage-inspired wallpaper.

have been bought or inherited, antiques come loaded with significance and meaning, making them powerful objects to have in the home.

Until recent times, vintage pieces (objects that are more than twenty years old but less than 100) and retro items (objects dating more specifically from about 1940 to 1989) were considered to be the poor relation of 'genuine' antiques, a knowing statement made by confident interior designers and cool homeowners. In today's interior-design trends, nothing could be hotter than mid-twentieth-century furniture and accessories.

It seems that we can't get enough of kitsch side tables, plastic kitchenware and other reminders of our recent past. While vintage and retro pieces may not always be a dazzling investment (although this is rapidly changing), they are an instant and economical way to add emotional depth and personal resonance to the home. When picked up at a charity shop, flea market or second-hand shop, mid-century finds can be inexpensive and cheerful. But they also serve a valuable decorative purpose; unlike 'proper' antiques, vintage and retro pieces and accessories often date from an era within our own living memory. This connects them directly with our childhood, reminding us of our cultural background, family life, friends, schooldays or misspent youth. Vintage objects are often witty, making us laugh or smile; when visitors spot a retro find in a friend's home, it often prompts happy reminiscences of their own.

The highly polished veneers, black lacquers and glossy chrome of art deco furniture create theatrical contrasts.

These enamel saucepans, produced by the Norwegian firm Cathrineholm from the 1950s until the company closed in 1970, make a bold, cheerful display and are as serviceable today as when they were made.

Your choice of vintage pieces can reveal your sense of humour or nostalgia, and what your background is. Far from being a statement of exclusivity, about high taste or specialist knowledge, vintage and retro finds are inclusive and democratic; they speak of a common past and shared experiences. A Regency wardrobe may confirm its owner's impeccable taste; a 1970s knitted toilet-roll cover makes everyone giggle, and declares that you don't take yourself too seriously.

Vintage pieces help to create interiors with quirkiness; above, a hanging bubble chair adds to the cheerful irreverence of the room. But retro can also be understated. Basing a scheme on a few quiet pieces, such as this sideboard and banquette (left), makes a subtle statement, helped along by a muted background and a pared-down aesthetic.

Mixing Up
the Generations

It is undeniable that there are some homes that at first glance appear to be chaotic but in which a mismatched look just seems to *work*; in which, despite a mix of styles, periods and colours, by some feat of 'magic' the rooms form a coherent whole. Mixing old and new, and different design aesthetics, can be tricky to pull off, but follow this set of rules behind the apparent anarchy and you'll have a home packed to the rafters with personality.

Tease Out a Unifying Colour

Disparate objects can relate to one another if they share a colour. The eye will naturally note and appreciate any unifying theme between objects, whether in a grouping of several items of one single colour, or in a variety of multicoloured pieces in which the same colour appears. In the display above, turquoise, white and orange are repeated in order to bring harmony to a kitsch selection of treasures.

Find Style Similarities

Some periods in design history share themes and motifs, despite being decades or even centuries apart. Many historical styles revived and copied earlier movements, so it's no surprise that they sit together comfortably. For example, the Arts and Crafts Movement of the late nineteenth century had its roots in medieval and Gothic styles, and pieces from these eras can look sensational together.

Arrange Similar Items In Groups

In a room containing a large number of small items, try to create cohesive groups of similar objects. Collections of model ships in bottles, for example, or of books or photographs, create more impact when massed together than when dotted about a room.

Look For Matching Shapes

Find touches of similarity. For example, a classic steel-and-leather Barcelona chair (designed by Ludwig Mies van der Rohe in 1929) has much in common with an eighteenth-century wooden scissors chair, both having X-shaped legs at the back only. A 1960s tripod floor lamp beautifully echoes the tapered shapes of both Shaker and late eighteenth-century furniture. Above, curvy X-shaped legs make natural partners of these two very different pieces.

Taming Technology

At the opposite end of the scale to period features is modern technology. Twenty-first-century necessities are everywhere in our living spaces. Life without mobile phones, washing machines, home entertainment systems and computers is almost unimaginable, but we would not necessarily choose to allow them to take centre stage in our interiors. Nevertheless it seems that in many homes television sets, for example,

Life is more pleasant when we are surrounded with things that are both useful and beautiful. Classic appliances, such as this vintage range oven, show that intelligent design and quality of construction rarely go out of fashion.

When not in use, this television is tucked away in a purpose-built but discreet wall unit, allowing conversation and socializing to focus on the centre of the room.

These rustic hand-built cupboards conceal a vast array of cutting-edge equipment without compromising the relaxed country style of the rest of the kitchen.

Collecting satisfies many different aspects of human nature, from a curatorial instinct to categorize objects (left) to our insatiable appetite for acquiring sets of related objects (below, left, and below).

Every compilation deserves a dedicated corner, whether it is a collection of museum-quality artefacts (as shown right) or flea-market treasure.

Burgeoning collections can soon take over a living space. Clever storage, shelving and display cases will prevent your prized possessions from becoming overwhelming.

and stated that the beauty an individual sees in an object, and the pleasure and satisfaction he or she gets from it, can never be properly gauged from its price tag. In other words, some of the most interesting and diverting collections can be of objects that have little or no inherent monetary value.

Creating a collection appeals to many different aspects of human nature. We can experience the treasure-hunting thrill of tracking down a particular item, and the librarian-like contentment derived from categorizing and sorting our finds. There's a happiness to be gained from becoming an expert on a specific topic or developing relationships with people who share your

An exquisite collection of old hand mirrors, interspersed with antique prints, makes an attractive and visually rhythmical display.

passions. Certain collections evoke feelings of nostalgia or connoisseurship; others might represent a canny investment for the future. But most of all, few things beat the undiluted joy of proudly displaying a collection so that others can share and appreciate your efforts and interests. A home with a collection, however small, is a deeply personal space.

Collections can be made of objects of all sorts and all sizes: small coins and classic model cars; colourful packaging; rare paintings; items relating to a specific era, event or person; limited editions of everyday items – there are no rules or boundaries. The only proviso is that the objects should have something in common with one another.

Cool Collections

Collecting is essentially a personal activity, but much of the pleasure is derived from showing the objects off and sharing them with others. Here are some instant ways to create a corner of curiosities or tabletop of treasures:

Use Old Shop or Museum Fittings

It can be tricky to display a collection to its greatest advantage. Take a leaf from a professional exhibitor's book, and use old shop fittings or museum cupboards to make the most of your treasures. Many of these charming cabinets have multiple glass sides or lift-up lids, allowing your collection to sparkle and shine. For a real cabinet of curiosities, add labels or tags to describe each artefact and record its history.

Use Dead Space

Collections often have most impact when they are sited in unexpected places. Around the home, look for traditionally 'dead' spaces that usually get ignored. Ideal for housing a treasured group of objects are the tops of kitchen cupboards; landings and hallways; alcoves and window ledges; empty spaces on bookshelves; downstairs cloakrooms; hearths; and large footstools.

Use Repetition to Create Visual Strength

Multiples of the same type of item make eye-catching collections. Use this natural repetition to create dazzling displays; a set of glass bottles, for example, or of mirrors (see photograph opposite), has much more impact as a group than when each is displayed in isolation.

Serve Up Your Collection

To create a contained display of small items, group them on a simple, unpatterned tray. This gives the collection importance and focus, but the tray also serves a practical purpose, making it possible to move your collection easily from surface to surface, and to keep delicate objects safe.

Hang Them All

Consider hanging your collection on a wall, even if the objects are unusual or non-domestic. Collections of quirky items, such as farming implements (see photographs pp. 96 and 162), hubcaps, enamel shop signs or old weathervanes, can really bring buzz to a blank section of wall.

Colours
and Fabrics

The creative impulse can extend well beyond the odd painting or picture; within the home, your interests and tastes can be expressed simply through your choice of fabrics and colours. For too long we have been encouraged to see our homes as investments and to remove from them all trace of personal taste. While a crazy colour scheme might not be the best decor if you're planning to sell, if you're staying put and want to create a real home it's time to stop thinking of market forces and start asking 'does this interior really reflect *me*?'

Designers and psychologists alike have long known that colours have a profound impact on us, but it's not quite as straightforward as one particular colour generating one single response. Most paint colours and wallpaper tones are subtle blends of many different shades and hues. A blue can contain elements of grey, green, pink; the variations are endless. So it would be simplistic to say that painting a home blue will make its occupants feel calm, as is often claimed. Within the vast range of blues that exist, there are blues that excite and blues that relax – a diversity of blues that evoke different emotions.

The only sure way to choose a colour is to try it. You'll be amazed by how instant your reaction to it is. We experience colour on a very basic level; if it feels wrong, no amount of time or 'getting used to it' will alter that sentiment. There is a knack to using colour in terms of decorating a home; balance and harmony are key elements in making a room feel comfortable. When redecorating a space

How to Match Colour and Fabric

Step One

Select your curtain or blind fabric. It will dictate the colours you use throughout the room.

Step Two

Pick out the background colour of the fabric and find a paint shade that matches. This is your wall colour.

Step Three

Identify a mid-tone colour from the fabric. Upholstery and flooring will look great in this shade (natural flooring, such as wood and stone, will also coordinate nicely).

Step Four

Pick out one of the brightest colours from the fabric and use this as an accent colour to lift the room. Repeat this on cushions, throws, trims and accessories.

Step Five

Use your curtain fabric in additional accents around the room, in cushions, lampshades and so on, as well as a coordinating fabric for depth; manufacturers often make sets of fabric designed to complement one another.

Opposite
Your choice of fabrics and wall colours says as much about your personality as do your pictures and other decorative decisions. Here, a subtle but clear bohemian, artistic aesthetic defines this bright sitting room.

Left
Strong colours, such as this deep red, don't have to be oppressive. During daylight hours, this large window and airy space more than compensate for the lack of reflective white. By night, deep shades create an enveloping cosiness.

Below
The playful, bold background colour and erratic pattern contrast wonderfully with the classical proportions of this reception room.

from scratch, it's useful to bear in mind the foolproof formula outlined on p. 89.

Fabric is remarkably important in creating a characterful home. It adds not just colour, but also visual warmth and texture. Vintage textiles can contribute that essential extra dimension of historical interest and appeal. The tried and tested way of incorporating fabric is through the use of soft furnishings, but antique or retro lengths of fabric make excellent wall art, too, stretched across wooden frames or trapped behind glass. Other opportunities to show off textiles and antique linens are offered by tablecloths, screens, footstools, bedspreads, laundry bags and lined wardrobes.

Opposite
In a home full of well-worn texture, natural materials and visual contrasts, fabric adds yet another layer of complexity and character.

Right, top
Stripes combine with *toile de Jouy* and other pictorial fabrics to communicate a reassuringly traditional feel. Society prints and Georgian antiques add to the air of refinement and gentility.

Right
Raw linen, fresh ticking and blocks of bright colour strike a contemporary note, suggesting a casual living space.

Bringing the Outside In

When we talk about character in homes, we are often referring to those elements that are man-made, such as period architectural features and paintings. But character can come from another source, one that is free, of unlimited availability and right on our doorsteps. Organic or natural elements will help homes to feel cosy and comforting. They bring touches of the outdoors into interiors, connecting us to our wider surroundings and creating an environment that feels both familiar and full of life.

Few of us live lives that are closely entwined with the countryside, and yet most people yearn for its pleasures. A deep-rooted part of our nature feels at home in natural surroundings, whether in the form of fresh flowers or an uninterrupted view. It's telling that, despite the fact that most of us live in cities or large towns, we like to surround ourselves with symbols, patterns and objects derived from nature. Our appreciation of floral fabrics, potted plants, seashells and driftwood shows that we can't quite cut ourselves off from our rural roots. We are also drawn to natural materials, such as wood, stone, wool and cotton. These slip seamlessly into our modern homes, bringing visual warmth, texture and a timeless quality that no man-made material can replicate.

Natural elements in the home can be employed to evoke a feeling of being linked to something larger; you don't just live in a house, you are also part of a wider environment. Somehow, connecting inside space with what's going on outdoors – on a balcony, in a garden large or small, or in

In this rural home, a glazed door, stone setts, timber cladding and exposed beams help to bridge the divide between indoor and outdoor space, creating a naturally welcoming entrance.

open countryside – makes for a spirited and well-rounded home. And if you have an active interest in some form of bucolic pleasure, from birdwatching or fossil hunting to horse riding or angling, it's great to show it off. A home that celebrates these wonderful pastimes will always be a rich and colourful place.

Opposite
A mix of animal artwork, floral compositions and outdoor scenes blends with exposed stonework and timber flooring in this rustic cottage.

Above
Motifs inspired by natural surroundings have long been employed to create ornate wallpapers and sumptuous fabrics.

Wood – here a significant presence, in the country kitchen table, mismatched chairs, recessed cupboard and sturdy beam – has a natural warmth and textural richness that help us to feel connected to our wider environment.

Natural Materials

Not so long ago, most homes were built by local builders following local traditions and using local materials. This is what's known as vernacular architecture, and it creates the wonderful variety of buildings we see up and down the country and around the world. Local trades would utilize the most freely available and robust natural materials to create homes with rich regional differences. One has only to think of thatched roofs, limestone rubble, dark Welsh slate and weatherboard cladding to be reminded of how diverse a nation's domestic architecture can be.

The diversity of organic materials, and the natural variety within each, mean that no two vernacular buildings are exactly the same. It's this individuality that creates character in a home.

When a building's form is beautiful in itself, keep the decor simple. A pale colour palette, slim furniture and folk art ensure that this space isn't compromised by its contents.

Using natural materials in this way achieves a number of things, all of which go to creating character. Not only does it result in buildings that are very specific to a geographical area, but also it creates variety between homes in the same region. Natural materials by their very essence are individual: no two handmade bricks or lumps of limestone are exactly the same; no two hand-hewn timber beams or marble worktops are ever quite alike. And that's what is so special. When we talk about a home having character, much of what we mean comes from the clever use of natural materials – the irregular beams, the handmade tiles or the locally fired bricks. It's not just a visual pleasure; there's a tactile quality, too, in the reassuring solidity of a vast oak beam or in the undulating surface of a chalky lime-plastered wall. These gentle, long-established materials are the bones and the flesh of a house, but they are now often overlooked in favour of modern, sleek lines and machine finishes.

Natural materials can easily be brought into a modern home or a newbuild. Cost is often cited as the reason not to use them – synthetic options can be cheaper – but with the added expense comes an infinitely more characterful home. Forget uPVC windows, veneers and laminate flooring; pastiche rarely matches the look or feel of the real thing. Natural building materials, such as reclaimed wood floorboards and stone worktops, are beautiful additions to the modern living environment. They're also more eco-friendly than conventional, carbon-heavy building materials, and they improve with age; the

Sleek lines and machine finishes would look out of place in this old farmhouse. There's real personality and tactile pleasure in the rough-hewn surfaces, foot-smoothed stone flags and undulating lime-plastered walls.

A scattering of natural materials can soften even the most minimalist of interiors. Aged terracotta adds a lovely, outdoorsy garden note to this elegantly austere corner.

bumps and scratches that are an inevitable part of wear and tear serve only to make natural materials more handsome and attention-grabbing.

Furnishings in such natural materials as wool, cotton, felt, jute and sisal add tactile softness and visual warmth beyond any synthetic equivalent. The snuggle factor of a woollen blanket and the crisp coolness of a linen sheet are a world away from polycotton mixes and scratchy nylon.

Opposite
A solid timber staircase and exposed roof joists create a feeling of timeless solidity, and contrast nicely with the sunflower bursts of the ornate golden mirrors.

Above
Rusticity and refinement coexist beautifully here: fine architectural details and French-style sofas sit comfortably alongside ancient timber supports, folk pieces and exposed rafters.

Outdoor
Life

A cloakroom overflowing with robust boots and country clothing (left) is a clear indication of a life spent outdoors more than in, while fishing rods, flies and tackle displayed on a charming antique wall stand (opposite) make their owner's favourite pastime clear for all to see.

If you enjoy the outdoors, and such activities as clay-pigeon shooting or horse riding, your home should reflect that. Many of the most exhilarating and good-natured homes proudly display this love of being in the open air. Boot rooms crammed with muddy wellies, fishing rods stuffed higgledy-piggledy in the umbrella stand: there's an energy and a rugged attitude that comes from living with these symbols of an active life.

Decor doesn't get more intimately domestic than a family of muddy wellies, or an ancient wooden cupboard crammed with fishing tackle, nets and reels. Even a utility room filled with the scent of leather boots and riding tack, or a hallway wicker basket overflowing with tennis rackets, walking sticks and umbrellas, speaks of outdoor life and family time. All these practical, precious items are not only useful, but symbolic, too.

A cheerful assortment of wellingtons and walking boots tangibly displays the outdoor pursuits that characterize the life of the family that lives in this home.

Riding equipment (above), tiny shoes (above, right) and vintage rackets: these much-loved personal objects convey more about their owners' pastimes than any shop-bought ornament.

Mother Nature's Mood Board

When it comes to design, human beings have always taken inspiration from the natural world. For as long as we have been painting walls, printing fabric and carving wood, we have mined the rich seam of symbolism and imagery that nature provides. Whatever your aesthetic, and whether you go for simple patterns or cheerfully blowsy chintz, there is an embarrassment of riches as regards nature-inspired home decor. Because of the variety on offer, it's easy to create a home environment that's uniquely yours. The combination of

A single huge leaf (opposite) and delicate sprigs on a floral bedspread and cushions (right) demonstrate the endlessly diverse ways in which the natural world informs and inspires interior decor.

fabrics, accessories and other floral accents will form a living space that's lively, original and, above all, distinctive. And remember, it's when you have a combination of qualities or features that distinguishes your home from another that you know you've created character.

Depending on the mood you want to generate, designs inspired by nature can be used in a multitude of ways. Prints of delicate sprigs of flowers conjure up traditional country-cottage chic. Bold, post-Impressionistic fabrics inspired by the art of the early twentieth-century Bloomsbury Group say something braver, more avant-garde. The romantic, heavily stylized forms of the Arts and Crafts Movement of the late nineteenth century strike a strong, medieval-inspired note, while the abstract floral designs of 1950s patterns create an evocative, retrospective feel.

Opposite, top and bottom
These displays of seemingly
unrelated objects are strongly
unified by a natural theme.
From the bird ornaments and
bright landscapes to the posies
of fresh flowers, each item has
been carefully selected to
create an organic collection.

Below and right
A floral raffia bag and stylized
patterns on a dainty dinner
service show that even the
smallest dash of flower design
can help to bring the outside in.

Almost any surface can be covered in
floral patterns and designs, but it's important
not to go overboard; there's a fine line
between flower power and flower *over*power.
Strong patterns have a potent effect, so it's
best to use bold fabrics and wallpaper
sparingly and to provide balance with plain
colours and neutral tones. Floral elements
can be brought in by other means, too; for
example, on a pretty set of vintage china
teacups or a small panel of stained glass.

Animal Magic

This whimsical doggy wallpaper strikes a well-judged balance between humour and sophistication. Horse prints add to the animal theme, creating a cheerful and characterful accent wall.

A fabulous display of caged birds provides an unmissable focal point in this room, but there's also an undercurrent of sea-themed accessories and fabrics dotted about.

Less often used than flowers and foliage as a source of inspiration, but equally effective, is the animal kingdom. There has been a recent resurgence in pictorial fabrics and wallpapers, and these can inject real humour and personality into a home. Many of us share our homes or outdoor spaces with treasured creatures, so it's fun to celebrate their presence with the odd animal print or accessory. Dogs, cats and other pets are not the only stars of this show; horses, chickens, cows, pigs and other farmyard friends are equally popular, turning traditional design subjects on their head and providing a rich source of quirky motifs for both country and city dwellers.

Different species have their own qualities, and when you incorporate specific animal motifs into your home you are making a clear design statement. No one could fail to pick up on the sharp contrast between a tiger print and a garden-bird fabric, so make sure your choices say something about the qualities you admire and appreciate. Beyond the usual prints and paintings, think about wallpapers and fabric, too. Whether you respond to the sophisticated hunting-lodge chic of Labrador prints or prefer cheerful sea-life motifs, there's a wide range of ways to bring the natural world into the home. To get the best effect, use repeating animal motifs sparingly; a boot room wallpapered with a pattern of ponies or a favourite chair covered

with pheasant-pattern fabric make a more effective statement than an entire animal-themed room.

Small collections of animal-shaped ornaments can have a big impact, too. A neat grouping of little ceramic figures on a bookshelf, for example, creates a pleasing cluster, while a single majestic statue can take centre stage on a mantelpiece or side table. Kitsch collections of porcelain birds, plastic animal toys or other car boot-sale finds can look sensational crowded on to a surface, adding a cheerful splash of colour or a wistful sense of nostalgia.

Opposite
A lively collection of antique bird prints fills the end wall of this quirky attic bedroom, tying in nicely with the porcelain birds on the mantelpiece.

Clockwise from top left
A sense of animation is exuded by groupings of animals, such as this little set of alert vintage hounds, flock of kitsch flea-market birds and quartet of specimen butterflies.

Objets Trouvés

While the direct translation of the French term *objets trouvés* is 'found objects', when we use the expression we are mostly thinking about those cherished finds we collect on beach strolls and woodland walks. Nature's flotsam and jetsam can create wonderful displays in the home. Most of us find such natural trinkets as seaside pebbles, sun-bleached driftwood, shiny conkers and intricate fossils too lovely to leave behind. These and other *objets trouvés* are essentially free ornaments, but their appeal goes well beyond cost. Nature is both full of repetitive patterns and delightfully random. Geometric forms occur time and time again in the natural world (think of the Fibonacci spiral of a shell, or the fractal leaves of a fern), and it's easy to see why we would want this order and elegance in our homes. But there is also the wonderful chaos of nature, which produces the crazed twists of hazel branches and the uniqueness of every sea-smoothed pebble. This individuality is deeply appealing, making no two *objets trouvés* ever quite the same.

There's poetry in our take-home treasures, too. As we gather driftwood during a seaside walk, we might wonder about where it has come from or the journey it has had before reaching our hands; the weathering and texture add to this mystery. Sculptural bones, skulls, shells, horns and discarded

Clockwise from opposite
The glorious forms of *objets trouvés*: animal skulls and horns, seed pods and driftwood, shells and starfish, pine cones, and sea-smoothed stones and twisted twigs – all of them serendipitous finds during nature walks and beachcombing.

antlers evoke both the poignant reality of life and a sense of renewal. Lost feathers, disused nests, seed pods, branches, leaves, pine cones: these simple items take on a new beauty and meaning when brought indoors. The British artist Andy Goldsworthy understands the power of nature's spoils; his sculptures are formed from found materials, including flowers, leaves, thorns, pine cones, stones and twigs. For Goldsworthy, the beauty of *objets trouvés* is not just in their diverse forms and colours, but also in their transience. 'Each work grows, stays, decays', he explains in the book *Hand to Earth* (1990). 'There is an intensity about a work at its peak.' In other words, one of the great charms of many *objets trouvés* is that they won't last forever. Knowing that they will eventually decay makes the enjoyment even sweeter.

In terms of character, not only do *objets trouvés* have their own stories to tell but also they act as constant reminders of the day we came across them. Every time we look at or handle these ephemeral riches we are transported back to a specific time and place – perhaps a family walk, a romantic stroll, a first date or a sad goodbye. Decorating the home with such profoundly personal belongings says much more about us as individuals than anything bought in a shop ever could.

Opposite, above and left
From curvy branches of corkscrew hazel to dried flowerheads and springtime catkins, salvaged twigs make instant sculpture that adds vertical interest and natural texture to any room.

Seaside Salvage

Beachcombing is one of life's most perfect pleasures, but what do you do with all the seaside salvage once you've hauled it indoors? Here are some eye-catching ways to incorporate coastal treasures into your home:

Tree Decorations

Shells, pretty pebbles and sea-smoothed pieces of glass make beautiful hanging decorations for a bouquet of twigs or a seasonal tree.

Table Centrepieces

Arranged in a group, stones, shells, nuts and large seeds make stunning table features, especially if you add a bit of sparkle from candlelight. To make a simple, rustic centrepiece, fill a zinc bucket or ceramic dish to the brim.

Mantelpiece Displays

Re-create the chaos of the beach by cramming a mantelpiece or shelf with various beachcombed textures. To create a seaside vignette, mix shells and driftwood of different shapes and sizes, and bring in other coastal elements, such as model boats or seascapes.

Tealight Holders

Sea urchins and clam shells make attractive holders for tea lights, and look great in large groups.

Specimen Trays

Emulate vintage natural-history collections by mounting your seaside finds in glass-fronted box frames or printers' trays. To add a curatorial touch, organize your finds in a logical order, such as by size or by colour.

Driftwood Decor

Repurpose sturdy pieces of driftwood into weathered decorations and hanging hooks. All sorts of handy objects can be created from well-worn wood: towel rails, candle sconces, signs, coat hooks, curtain poles, tie-backs, frames for mirrors and paintings, wall art, free-standing sculpture, lamp bases, screens ...

Dinner-party Pieces

Attach small shells to twine or ribbon and tie around crisp white napkins; use hand-painted pebbles as nameplates or tablecloth weights.

Feathers

Use decorative feathers as you would flowers: set large feathers in a generous vase, create a posy from a compact collection of small ones. Make feather wreaths and delicate bunting.

Flower Power

A pot of lily of the valley and a bouquet of tulips give this otherwise unadorned corner a welcome lift of colour and heady scent.

An all-white white interior is made less stark thanks to a single vase of pink-tinged roses, which adds much-needed colour and contrast.

A sunny window sill makes the perfect miniature garden for all manner of perfumed plants, kitchen herbs and potted blooms.

It's official: nature is good for us. Scientific studies have repeatedly proved that feeling connected to the natural world not only helps to alleviate stress and promotes relaxation, but also improves our overall sense of well-being, physical health and feelings of happiness. It should come as no surprise, then, that homes that embrace natural elements tend to make the most enjoyable, homely and welcoming domestic environments.

One of the quickest ways to bring the outside in is to fill the home with living plants and fresh flowers. Garden writer and designer

A floral welcome: a shaggy fern and ingenious flower 'chandelier' soften this clean-lined entrance hall, providing a transitional link between home and garden.

Noel Kingsbury hit the nail on the head when he wrote in *The Indoor Gardener: Creative Displays for Every Home* (1994): 'Living with plants involves sharing your home ... with organisms that need air, water and food just like ourselves.' It might seem odd to suggest that the reason we like living with house plants is that they depend on us for survival, but the human instinct to care for and nurture living things is one of our strongest drives. There's a great deal of pleasure to be gained from seeing a plant flourish thanks to the love and attention we've lavished on it.

That's not the only reason we bring floral displays into our homes, however. They also contribute welcome bursts of brightness, particularly appreciated at times when we're lacking a little colour in our own lives. Indoor plants provide a link between interior and exterior space, a connection that is all the more important when the weather is against us. Scented flowers can fill a room with glorious natural perfume. Plants, because they're mutable, also bring a sense of dynamism and movement to a room: no two days are ever exactly the same. And, because plants and cut flowers come in all shapes, shades and sizes, we can use them as a painter would a palette of paints, to add unique form and colour to any interior scheme.

Right, top and bottom
The ever-changing form and colour of living plants and cut flowers bring movement and energy to a room.

Talking Scents

A sweet-smelling home is a welcoming one. We seldom take scent into account when planning our homes, and yet it has a profound effect both on our mood and on the general ambience. Aromas can be uplifting, calming, sensual and even appetite-arousing, but you might want to think about alternatives to a chemical-laden can of air freshener. The scents that belong in a characterful home are those that come from natural sources: a waft of woodsmoke, the intense sweetness of honeysuckle or the zesty tang of fresh herbs.

Certain scents evoke memories or the changing seasons. Oily pine needles and orange peel are evocative of a family Christmas; citronella and lavender speak

Left and below
We experience our living spaces through all our senses, including that of smell. Highly fragrant tea roses or sharply zingy citrus fruits are among the many sources for a naturally perfumed environment.

Opposite
Open fires provide natural scents that are perhaps the most redolent of a secure, happy home. Cedar and fruitwood logs, pine cones and rosemary kindling will all contribute to producing a richly aromatic smoke.

of summer days; and the just-laundered freshness of children's clothes or the leathery warmth of a riding saddle are uniquely comforting. There's no doubt that our sense of smell and our sense of home are inextricably linked. Certain aromas – floor polish, perhaps, or freshly brewed coffee – can transport us to a different time or place, or create an instant atmosphere of homeliness and comfort. Smell is thought to be our 'oldest' sense; newborns know the scent of their mothers from birth, and rely on their sense of smell to differentiate between familiar and unfamiliar. It's no wonder that aromas release such powerful emotions.

Scents can bring therapeutic and sensual pleasure into our homes. From the stimulating freshness of orange oil to the intoxicating headiness of lilies, nature offers an almost unending store cupboard of fragrances.

A Sweet-smelling Home

A home that smells good *feels* good. There is nothing nicer than a kitchen filled with the warm smell of baking, or a laundry room bursting with lavender freshness. Rather than masking bad odours with artificial fragrances, bring natural, non-toxic perfumes and aromas into your home. Many of life's day-to-day activities – cooking, baking, washing, cleaning – bring their own delightful fragrances, especially if you stick to natural ingredients. Here are four of nature's top performers.

Lavender

The stalwart of a naturally scented home, lavender offers many benefits, including being antibacterial, relaxing and insect-repelling. The essential oil and flowers of this versatile plant can be used in cooking (for example, in cupcakes, ice-cream or shortbread), in cleaning materials (in wash-day linen water or fabric softener), in bathing water and in bedtime rituals.

Lemon

Another wonderfully versatile ingredient, lemon can be used as a flavouring, a degreaser and an antiseptic. It is also a powerful deodorizer and disinfectant, and it bleaches stains and repels insects. As a scent, lemon tends to invigorate, making it an ideal fragrance for daytime spaces and cleaning products.

Rose

A gentler fragrance than lavender and lemon, but no less useful, rose is both soothing and antiseptic. It also has many culinary uses, as a flavouring for teas, jams, sweets and waters. Dried, its petals make an excellent filler for aromatic bags and sachets, and its oil can be added to distilled water to create a calming room spray (use about 80 drops per 100ml/4 fl. oz of water).

Vanilla

Both delicious and aromatic, vanilla triumphs as a spice and a housekeeping favourite. While many qualities have been ascribed to it, such as being an aphrodisiac and an antioxidant, its appeal for most of us lies in its comforting association with home baking. Its aroma adds a homely infusion to anything from scented sugar to votive candles and even home-made bath salts.

The Devil's In the Detail

It is always gratifying when someone takes pride in their work. And, from simple rustic pieces of furniture to ornate rococo mirrors, items that demonstrate real workmanship and care are a joy to live with. Quality and craftsmanship are key ingredients in a characterful home. While a cheap and cheerful interior makeover can have an instant effect, it's not long before the cracks begin to show. It's time to return to basics.

'Have nothing in your houses that you do not know to be useful or believe to be beautiful.' This quotation from William Morris (from *Hopes and Fears for Art*, first published in 1882) has become so overused that its important message has lost much of its power. And yet we ignore it at our peril. The nineteenth-century artist was asking us to think carefully about the objects we select for our homes; in particular, we should treasure those elements often missing in modern manufacture, such as traditional skills, personality and a deep sense of craftsmanly pride.

Morris was devoted to the notion of craftsmanship. In an age when industrialization and mass production were racing ahead, his belief in the importance of good-quality, handmade home furnishings and decorations seemed out of touch. He wanted people to cherish and celebrate human endeavour and skill; with so many goods being produced by machines, it was difficult for workers to experience any creativity, freedom or skill in their daily working lives. Morris was determined that centuries of learned crafts and skills, such as weaving and woodcarving, would not be lost. He argued that the ideal home didn't just suit handcrafted decoration, it also actually *needed* it; shoddy, mass-produced furnishings contributed nothing. It was time to get back to high-quality materials, honest construction and graceful design.

Morris's beliefs have proved profoundly influential. Over the past century we've learned much about the limitations of a flat-pack world, one in which everything is

Quality always shines through. With its Shaker-style unfussiness and attention to detail, this handcrafted high-backed chair is both dateless and elegant.

Characterful homes often embrace craftsmanship and the finest raw materials in everything from fixtures and fittings to finishing touches.

Craftsmanship doesn't have to mean complexity. Often it's the down-to-earth, honest pieces, such as this writing desk and rush-seat chair, that show off a maker's expertise.

made to the same mould. It would seem that, for all the obvious benefits and convenience of mass production, nothing can better the beauty, elegance and sheer humanity of home-made treasures and well-crafted pieces. In relation to buildings and their furnishings, the conclusion is clear: a home containing only off-the-shelf, mass-produced items will always lack soul.

Both home-made and handcrafted pieces will add character to a living space, but it's important to distinguish between the two. Home-made objects are often full of charm and homely personality; we make them with love and affection, rather than with perfection in mind, and this gives them their unique quality. Craftsmanship, in contrast, involves skill, specialism and acquired knowledge. It's about being proficient and able, and producing objects of high quality. The distinction between the two is the difference between a cheerful crocheted throw and an exquisitely carved table leg. And yet, for all these contrasts, home-made and hand-crafted pieces have much in common, especially when it comes to helping to create character.

Quality and Character

We live in a world obsessed by quick fixes. Whether this comes from the fact that we have less spare time than we once had, or whether we simply have less patience than previous generations, there are few of us who do not like quick answers to difficult questions. When it comes to interiors, one of the ways in which this attitude manifests itself is in the popularity of home-makeover television

Below, left
It's always refreshing to see evidence of a carpenter's skill and high-quality materials. Extra-wide floorboards, profuse use of timber and age-old construction give this bathroom timeless appeal.

Below
Homespun functional objects can have bags of charm. Crocheted throws, a handmade blanket box and patchwork soft furnishings all add to the relaxed, lived-in feel of these cosy rooms.

Surrounding ourselves with handmade objects reminds us that we are all creative beings, capable of innovative thought and playful productiveness.

shows. And there is much to recommend them. In just the short time it takes to watch a programme, we see a shabby, unloved room transformed into a highly styled interior complete with new furniture, accessories and 'artwork'. But, impressive as the results are in terms of the sheer graft that's gone into transforming a home so quickly, one always gets the niggling feeling that all isn't quite as it seems. Not only do makeovers leave the rooms looking like personality-free furniture showrooms, but also one often wonders how long the finishes and furnishings will last, especially those that were knocked off quickly.

It's easy to criticize TV makeover shows, and we do have a lot to thank them for. They have brought interior design and home decoration to the forefront; never before have so many people been passionate about making their homes comfortable, cosy and visually coordinated places. But perhaps it's time to divert the focus from the quick fix, and turn it to quality instead.

Home ...
It's a Feeling

When we try to define what we mean by
'character' in a house, we have to think
about what makes a home feel 'right'.
Nothing is more frustrating than materials
or workmanship that don't live up to
expectations. The home should be a place
that supports and nurtures our spirit, not one
that reminds us how unreliable and unsafe
the world might be. Badly made, crudely
designed home furnishings and fixtures don't
just look unappealing, they also have the
power to frustrate, annoy and exasperate.
We use most of the items in our homes with

Right, top
Ancient and antique pieces
add another layer to character
and craftsmanship,
demonstrating not just the
beauty of well-made objects
but also their inherent longevity.

Right
High-quality pieces rarely
need embellishment. These
handsome chairs and dining
table have more than enough
presence to fill this vast space,
without requiring ornate
details or garish decoration.

Good-quality materials can make a quietly elegant backdrop. Antique wooden panelling provides an ideal canvas for the trinkets and treasures that accumulate over the years.

If you keep costs down with a plain bathtub and other basics, you can splurge on the details, such as classic bath mixers, marble splashbacks and delft tiles.

such regularity that, if something doesn't work well or feels shoddily put together, as in the case of a wonky chair, a badly fitted door, or a cheaply made throw that feels rough to the touch, it can really affect how we feel in our living environment.

We experience our homes not just through seeing them, but also through touching and using them. The objects with which we furnish our interiors need to be up to the task, ready to take all that family life can throw at them. One of the best ways to ensure that is to select good-quality materials and to buy or make things that work, are well made and will last. In his book about why it matters to get things right, *The Craftsman* (2008), the American-born scholar Richard Sennett comes to the conclusion that 'all craftsmanship is quality-driven work ... The aspiration for quality will drive a craftsman to improve, to get better rather than get by.'

The details are very often what clinches the matter. The dovetail joints, the neat stitching, the extra flourishes that turn a mundane item into a thing of beauty: great craftsmanship is never meretricious. In our homes, we are often extravagant with the big items but forget the small details – the taps, the knobs, the handles, the trims – and yet these are the very things that make all the difference. Estate agents often talk about 'finish', and it's surprising how influential this can be when it comes to forming an impression of someone's home. A poorly finished property might be just as superficially comfortable as a well-finished one, but househunters will

Not all antiques have to be kept immaculate. Inexpensive Victorian tables and chairs have been pressed into service in this artist's studio, providing solid and attractive seating and workbenches.

equate botched DIY jobs and shoddy fixtures with more serious problems.

The objects we use in our homes need to be fit for purpose; a home that contains things purely for show cannot be a characterful one. Good design has always involved someone identifying a need, and then designing and making an object that fulfils that need. Add a touch of creative brilliance to the process, and the result is an object that's likely to please generation after generation. 'The simplest way of defining a design classic is that it is 98 per cent common sense', noted the designer and retailer Terence Conran in an interview for the Coutts website in 2010. 'What makes the subject so interesting is the other 2 per cent, what you may call aesthetics. Many products are demonstrably good. But those with that extra 2 per cent have a magic ingredient that places them in another category altogether.'

Opposite
Simple plywood dining chairs with metal legs were first produced in the mid-twentieth century and have been copied ever since, showing that good design and functionality are not the preserve of antiques.

Right
If you can't buy it, build it. This striking, handmade four-poster bed provides a focal point in the bedroom and makes the space unique.

Being Honest

The drive for quality in design includes honesty of construction and truth to materials. This might sound like pompous designer-speak, but the idea is simple: the most satisfying objects are those made not to deceive. Home furnishings that appear to be older, of better materials or of slicker design than they really are almost always look fake. Artificially aged 'shabby chic' furniture, for example, rarely has the same appeal or charm as a genuinely worn piece. The aesthetic is broadly similar, yet we instinctively know the difference. When

Opposite, left
Few materials are more characterful than bare wood. No two knots, grain patterns or patinas are ever identical, guaranteeing a room's individual personality.

Opposite, right
Why buy artificially aged furniture when you can pick up the genuine article for the same price or less? This down-to-earth old pine cupboard fits perfectly with the prettily plain Shaker aesthetic in this room.

As can be seen in such details as the fine casting of this iron hob grate and the exquisite carving of the marble surround, the Georgians and Victorians loved to show off what could be achieved through human skill and technological innovation.

The owners of this historic kitchen have been careful not to strip the character from the wonderfully varied bricks and hand-hewn beam by overzealous cleaning.

there's no heritage or story behind the façade, 'distressed' furniture and ornaments can resemble stage scenery. The same problem occurs in a home filled with cheap reproductions; from a distance these counterfeits pass muster, but up close the illusion falls apart. That's not to say that all reproductions are a waste of time. If the quality of construction and the design are true to the original, a modern reproduction can slip nicely into a personality-packed home. Today's Lloyd Loom chairs, for example, are still made using traditional methods and techniques developed in the early twentieth century, and are as elegant and sturdy as those produced a century ago.

Striving for honesty is at the heart of all good home restoration work. Only a few decades ago, the philosophy behind most conservation work was to make it look as if it had always been there. While on one level this makes sense, conservationists now take the approach that it's better to be truthful about repairs and replacements, and to celebrate them as part of the building's history. The same high-quality materials are used, but there's no attempt to age or weather them artificially, so that the building and its physical history can be 'read' easily.

This little vignette shows the variety of materials we employ in our homes. The sleek lines of a 1930s filing cabinet and metal lamp columns contrast elegantly with the carved flourishes on an antique wooden mirror and the silky coolness of fired pottery.

Left
Distressed furniture adds
instant antique charm in
this traditional context. The
delightfully battered chest of
drawers adds a powerful layer
of visual texture and touch
appeal without dominating
the space.

Below
In this well-worn dining room
no attempt has been made to
cover up the building's bumps
and scratches. The worn
flagstones, heavily overpainted
doors and mottled lime plaster
all add to the palpable sense of
history and human occupation.

In practical terms, always try to fill your home with objects that are what they claim to be. Forget fakes and copies, and go for the genuine article. Laminate flooring versus real wood; plastic 'marble' surfaces versus solid stone slabs; polyester sheets versus crisp cotton: it's not difficult to see that the real deal usually comes out on top. It may initially cost more to invest in high-quality, honest materials, but they almost always last longer and wear better than their counterfeit cousins.

In the contemporary home this concept can also be applied to modern materials. Some of the most exciting, dynamic and characterful modern living spaces are those that embrace the natural qualities of the materials of which they are made, such as polished concrete, moulded plastics, brushed steel, cast resin and vast expanses of glass; these materials shouldn't be disguised as something else. There are few inherently 'good' or 'bad' materials (apart from those that are unsustainable, unethical or harmful). Rather, it is their appropriate use that matters.

Buying Quality on a Budget

The higher the quality of materials or level of workmanship, the steeper the price tag. Right? Well, not always. You *can* get quality on a budget; just follow three simple rules:

Treasure Hunt

Thanks to salvage yards, thrift shops and auction websites, high-value materials and furniture can be picked up at reduced prices, especially if you're prepared to search. Styles go in and out of fashion, so if you're canny about what you buy you can grab previously expensive materials for bargain prices. The recent trend for stripped country pine, for example, left furniture made from more expensive and long-lasting woods, such as mahogany and oak, languishing in antiques shops at heavily discounted prices. It's only when attempting to buy a chunk of new mahogany from a timber yard that one realizes the true value of these pieces.

Go for Details

It's a time-honoured property developer's approach: spend your budget on the details that matter and that get the most handling. A reclaimed door doesn't cost much, but it will feel infinitely grander if it sports an exquisite antique or handmade handle and escutcheon. A simple wooden kitchen sparkles when it's embellished with high-quality hinges, worktops and drawer handles. A plain white, off-the-shelf bathroom suite can look a million dollars with top-end taps.

Don't Be Sniffy About Seconds

High-end manufacturers have to be ruthless about the finish of their products; no blip or bump can be tolerated, and many items find their way into clearance. Use this pursuit of quality to your advantage by snapping up seconds. The odd mark or imperfection is a small price to pay for furnishing your home with well-made, beautifully designed classics at a knock-down price.

The Maker's Mark

If you've created something of quality, you'll want to shout about it. It's no coincidence that makers of fine furniture and ornaments have always marked their creations with some kind of signature. The message is clear: they are pleased with the result of their labours and are prepared to put their name to it. And so, when you are looking for pieces for your home, one way to aim for quality is to look for some evidence of the person who made it. This could be in the form of a signature,

Opposite, left
This hand-painted glass panel, with its stylized flowers and swooping swallow, transforms a functional little window into an enchanting, deeply individual decorative panel.

Opposite, right
Even the most workaday corner can be enhanced by pieces that have been designed by a craftsperson and built by hand. Here, a chic mid-twentieth-century desk and chair make a handsome pairing in this calming study.

Right
As can be seen from this 1950s armchair, the most visually exciting pieces of furniture combine functional design and common sense with creative flair.

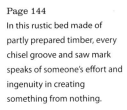

Page 144
In this rustic bed made of partly prepared timber, every chisel groove and saw mark speaks of someone's effort and ingenuity in creating something from nothing.

Page 145
A maker's pleasure often shines through in the design and execution of an object. This breathtakingly elegant walnut chair by the American designer Norman Cherner is now regarded as an icon of 1950s craftsmanship and slick innovation.

a factory mark, a maker's mark or a symbol. For example, the woodcarver and furniture-maker Robert Thompson, who was part of the 1920s revival of craftsmanship, carved a small mouse on every piece he created. Now an instantly recognizable hallmark of his work, Thompson's signature mouse has come to represent quality and dedication to a craft. And when it comes to investing, named pieces are a safe bet. Shrewd buyers who purchased work by such innovative modern designers as Ludwig Mies van der Rohe, Charles and Ray Eames and Ron Arad are now seeing their pieces rocket in value.

Even unsigned or anonymous pieces can give clues about their creators, by reflecting their tastes and personal aesthetics or simply by demonstrating their care, skill and practicality. When you truly examine a handmade treasure, whether a marriage quilt or a carved newel post, you'll see that every stitch or chisel mark represents someone's time, effort and love. Machine-made pieces can never possess this delightful human quality. If you've made something yourself, even better. Every time you look at it you'll be reminded of all your hard work and dedication. Often in life, and especially at work, we do just enough to get by. Craftsmanship and making things by hand are about more than that; they might be practical activities but they're not just a means to an end. Home-made and handcrafted items are about the maker being engaged in a task and doing a good job for the sheer pleasure of it. That kind of passion never fails to come through in the results.

Bespoke Pieces

Sometimes, no matter how hard you search, it can feel as if you will never find an absolutely perfect piece of furniture or matching fixture. And whether you need a cupboard for an awkward corner or want to mark a celebration with a special object, commissioning a bespoke item of furniture or handmade fittings can be a lovely way to bring originality and one-off charm into your home. It can be very satisfying to know that you have something truly unique: for example, quirky handmade kitchen units, ornate ironwork, hand-blocked wallpaper or one-off light fittings. In the same way that a made-to-measure suit fits the wearer beautifully, a commissioned piece will slide gracefully into your living space. It's not an inexpensive venture, however, so it pays to do some research.

Alcoves and tricky corners often need bespoke solutions, such as this hand-built bookcase (opposite), in order to make the most of the space. There is pleasure in knowing that a piece created to solve a particular problem is also unique to your living space.

A craftsworker can turn your wildest design ideas into reality. This wooden banister (right, top), which looks as if it has come straight out of a fairy tale, was clearly constructed specifically for this staircase from salvaged branches and logs. The more conventional, but no less skilled, handcrafted wrought-iron banister (right) has turned a winding staircase into a work of art.

Before you approach potential makers or manufacturers, have a general idea of what you'd like. Think about dimensions, materials and elements of the design. Nothing is fixed at this stage, but it's useful to have some starting points for discussion. Visit the showroom and workshops if possible; it's a real treat to see traditional techniques being kept alive in the twenty-first century, and it can be a rich source of inspiration. You'll also need to have a very clear idea of your budget. Discuss money as soon as possible, so that everyone's expectations can be managed. The design process and the manufacture are often charged out separately, as a craftsworker may need to be compensated for any time spent on creating drawings (especially if you don't go ahead

Invest in the most visible pieces. This simple, newly panelled room has been brought to life with a fitting bespoke fire surround, adding focus and structure to the space.

Opposite
You can commission almost any item for your home – hand-built kitchen cupboards painted the exact shade you want (top), wrought-iron roof ties (bottom left) or a one-off fireside set (right) – and create an environment that's uniquely yours.

with the project). Clarify the fee structure as early in the proceedings as possible.

The design stage is an exciting one, in which both you and the maker can have a creative input, so use this time to put forward all your ideas and suggestions. When both of you are happy that you can proceed, get everything in writing. Make sure the contract includes details of materials, dimensions, methods of manufacture, timescales, costs and payment terms, refunds and any guarantees. It might all sound daunting, but in reality most clients are delighted with their bespoke pieces and thoroughly enjoy the process from start to finish.

Kitchens readily lend themselves to bespoke pieces, such as clever storage for an awkward corner (left), or shelves and units designed to fit a very specific space (below, left). This crockery cupboard (below) was created in the early nineteenth century to fit a space by the side of a fireplace.

Celebrating Craftsmanship

It's easy to bring craftsmanship and quality into your home, even on a tight budget. Well-made, lovingly crafted pieces of furniture and decoration not only make your home individual but also imbue it with sophisticated but homely character.

Do Your Homework

Become knowledgeable about a specific style, movement or maker famed for his or her craftsmanship. You'll soon start to recognize their work, and will be more likely to spot a bargain at a car boot sale or auction.

Celebrate Craft Techniques

Reject the uniformity of flat-pack furniture and learn to love the originality of one-offs and homely treasures. Look for pieces that hold signs of the person who made them, whether it's thumbprints in a pottery jug or chisel grooves in woodwork.

Don't Follow Fashion

Buy things for your home that are ageless rather than fashionable. Trends die out as quickly as they are born, and you could be left with a home that looks dated. A classic chesterfield sofa, for example, will fit almost any design scheme and will withstand the rigours of family life.

Look for Investment Pieces

Regardless of trends, good-quality items will always hold their value and will give you years of pleasure into the bargain. Whether you opt for Georgian furniture or 1960s retro pieces, look for quality of materials, durability, expert craftsmanship and touches of originality.

Support Local Craftsworkers

Whether for a bespoke wardrobe or a commissioned ceramic dish, there's a rich seam of twenty-first-century craftsmanship waiting to be mined. Forget village-hall fêtes; instead look for high-end design at local studios and workshops, craft fairs and galleries. Look into commissioning fixtures and fittings for the home, not just ornaments and furniture.

A Sense of Surprise

Interior design can be a bit po-faced.
In the pursuit of cutting-edge trends,
we sometimes forget what homes should
really be about, namely laughter and love.
And while we should always take good
design seriously, this doesn't mean that
we have to take *ourselves* too seriously.
Some of the most enjoyable homes are
those that revel in humour or gentle
irony, visual quirks and interesting
juxtapositions. When exuberance and
surprise are allowed through the door,
character flows in with them.

The word 'character' is such a slippery fellow. When we use it to describe a person, it could signify various traits: moral goodness (as in the expression 'a man of good character'), originality, great wit or distinctiveness. We also use it when someone is playful, funny or downright cheeky; the phrase 'Oh, she's *such* a character' springs to mind. It is the same with homes. As discussed throughout this book, 'character' in interiors can refer to a number of qualities, from a strong sense of history and heritage through to such abstract notions as creativity, originality and warmth. In this final chapter, we will see that character can also come from expressing the side of human nature that is so often ignored in the home: our sense of humour and playfulness.

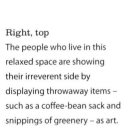

Right, top
The people who live in this relaxed space are showing their irreverent side by displaying throwaway items – such as a coffee-bean sack and snippings of greenery – as art.

Right
This flat-pack plywood moose's head takes a traditional hunting-lodge interior design motif and subverts it into something distinctly more playful and animal-friendly.

Humour and the Home

Homes work hard for us. They shelter us, protect us and nurture us. But they can do even more, if we know how to harness their potential. Homes can raise a smile and constantly surprise us. If we've had a bad day, there's nothing better than living in a place that lifts our spirits and reminds us of the lighter side of life. Humour can come from a wide variety of sources, such as paintings, photos, ornaments, furniture and even colour, but its use in the home needs a subtle hand.

Left
There's Malibu-beach madness at work in this gorgeously girlie interior. The ice-cream-van colours, flamboyant furniture and plastic flamingo tell us that the owner doesn't like to take herself too seriously.

Opposite
Even in the most traditional, classic interior there is room for the ridiculous. A laughing theatrical mask and mannequin's hands add a note of dark humour to this intimate attic space.

A Sense of Surprise 155

A home doesn't have to make people laugh out loud to be humorous. Sometimes just placing an object out of context, such as this boat suspended from the ceiling, provides wry originality.

Humour often arises from something being out of context. If we are not expecting quirky salvage, say, or retro adverts, charming typography or surprising ornaments in a home, their presence will surprise and delight us. They may also play with traditional notions of what an interior should look like. From a visitor's point of view, a home that doesn't take itself too seriously is deeply welcoming: a humourless, too-perfect interior can be intimidating. If we sense that our host has a playful side, we can relax, loosen up and feel at home.

Many interior designers swear by the dictum, 'Always have something ugly in a room'. By this they mean that a room should feature something tattered, humorous or just plain weird in order to create a conversation piece and avoid the 'showroom effect'. A stag's head with a hat on it, a marble bust wearing sunglasses, a battered old armchair ... it could be anything, so long as it's unique or mischievous.

In an otherwise restrained interior this horse is a wonderfully flippant statement, giving guests an instant talking point and providing cheerful focus.

Tiny touches can have a big impact. This risqué mermaid bottle opener gives its owners a giggle every time they use it, and adds a welcome splash of yellow to an otherwise green and blue palette.

Surprising
Salvage

Giving a new purpose to an old object can have exciting results. Here, a pair of weather-beaten shutters propped nonchalantly against a stone wall makes a fantastic magazine rack.

Opposite, top
A rough-and-ready timber pallet has been transformed into a plate rack, its coarse texture and form fitting in perfectly in this unusual but stylish kitchen made from reclaimed materials.

Opposite, bottom
The inherent uniqueness of salvage makes it an ideal candidate for the 'mix and match' aesthetic, as in the case of this reclaimed timber dining table teamed with industrial-inspired aluminium chairs. Stripped floorboards and a restrained colour palette add to this city-chic location.

People have always scavenged building materials to use in new construction. This 'waste not want not' philosophy was applied in the Roman colonies of Gaul and Britain, where builders used stones from damaged or abandoned local buildings in imposing defensive city walls; and in medieval England, Roman bricks and columns were reused in great new churches. But it was in the 1960s that the salvage industry really began to grow, with enterprising builders and architects coming to realize that much of our built heritage was ending up in skips. Traditional building materials and architectural antiques were the first to catch people's attention, especially that of house restorers who were looking to reinstate period features that had been lost. As discussed in the first chapter of this book (pp. 18–43), reinstating these crucial architectural fittings proved a sure-fire way of adding character to even the most picked-clean of period homes.

It wasn't long, however, before adventurous homeowners and off-the-wall designers started to see greater, more creative potential for reclaimed materials. This 'salvage look' is now one of the most exciting and eccentric forms of interior expression, using everyday objects to produce fantastical, unique interiors. Mixing up the periods, turning function on its head, and creating beauty from often mundane or redundant objects break all the conventional rules of interiors. Rooms kitted out with reclaimed materials are inherently fun precisely because they do not follow any rules. No two salvage-furnished interiors can ever be the

In a whimsical take on a traditional blanket-box arrangement, the owners of this retro bedroom have brought together a reclaimed tobacco crate, homely throws and a kitsch erotic painting that refers to the blankets beneath it.

This curious collection of finds harmonizes thanks to a shared palette. Vintage plant markers, old chemist's jars, a life-study model and a cast hand create a fanciful but visually balanced display.

same, as reclaimed materials are infinitely varied. From cruise-ship chairs, church pews and art nouveau tiles to industrial worktops, neon nightclub lighting and delicate wrought-iron grilles, the potential for originality and reinvention is huge.

Such salvage pioneers as Mark and Sally Bailey, who established Baileys Home and Garden in Bridstow, Herefordshire, in 1984 and have written several books on interiors, have used reclaimed materials to create a new aesthetic, mixing up retro and rustic, industrial and recycled objects. The Baileys devise storage from fishing baskets and wine crates on wheels, lighting from wine bottles and empty kilner jars, tumblers from recycled tyres, toothbrush holders from recycled oak blocks, splashbacks from driftwood and delicate vases from vintage milk bottles. It works, not only because their design sensibility is original and creative, but also because many of the household items they create have a wry sense of humour behind them or constitute a curious twist on the everyday. There's character in spades, and it's mostly thanks to the fact that, in each object, there is clear evidence of an individual's guiding intelligence and a delightful defiance of conformity.

Vintage tins and food-themed ephemera from many countries make an eye-catching and colourfully nostalgic backdrop in this retro-inspired kitchen. Early twentieth-century advertising, with its bright graphics and confident design, can look great in highly contemporary living spaces, too.

Have Fun
with Salvage

Reclaimed materials have endless possible uses and
decorative potential; the only limit is your imagination.
Here are some suggestions for making the most of them.

Little and Large

Oversized or miniature pieces
of salvage can create attention-
grabbing centrepieces or
talking points (see pp. 164–67).
Furniture and fittings from
industrial, church or public
settings, for example, are often
larger than those made for
domestic environments. Make
a bold statement with an
oversized stepladder, a large
canteen table, a platform clock,
a dance-hall mirror or some
stage scenery.

Play at Shops

Commercial salvage, such as
enamel advertisements, shop
signs, neon lights, display
cabinets and chemist's or
sweetshop jars, can look
sensational in the home. Not
only do they inject retro
appeal but also they add a
touch of playful make-believe
to an interior.

Life Outside

Blur the boundary between
outdoors and indoors by
setting garden or farming
salvage in the home. Antique
gardening tools, stone statues,
large terracotta pots and
railway benches are among
the 'outdoor' items and furniture
that transfer particularly
successfully to an interior.

Mix It Up

Salvage defies an organized approach. Embrace its spirit of eclecticism and mix up eras and styles to create a dynamic, idiosyncratic interior. Reclaimed materials are usually well constructed and designed, and such items as old laundry tubs, zinc hospital sinks, Georgian floorboards, post-war kitchen units and oak pub fittings can fit in comfortably in a modern home.

Old Dogs, New Tricks

Change the function or purpose of a salvaged item to create something novel. Almost anything goes: turn shutters into wall panelling or magazine racks (see photograph p. 158), railway trolleys into coffee tables, taps and tools into rows of hooks, shoe lasts into table feet or candle holders, and fruit crates into bedroom storage. Even battered old lockers make handsome and useful repositories for favourite finds.

Playing
with Scale

Humour in the home doesn't mean laugh-out-loud funny; rather, the effect should be good-naturedly unconventional. One of the most effective ways of achieving this is to play with scale. Both miniature and oversized pieces do something magical to interiors: their presence upsets the traditional balance, but in a way that makes us feel excited or intrigued.

Most children love miniature things. Kids often feel small and powerless, and so revel in scenarios and objects that make them feel like giants and allow them physically to dominate their own environment. That thrill doesn't leave us as we grow into adulthood, but rarely do we get to experience it. And yet, tiny objects are full of charm and character. We admire the painstaking craftsmanship that has gone into creating a diminutive version of a full-size item, hence the appeal of the miniature 'apprentice piece' made to test the skill of a novice craftsworker. We also enjoy the visual humour that comes from placing a tiny chair or chest of drawers on a mantelpiece or shelf. But often, much as with doll's houses, the pleasure comes from the

A vastly over-sized sculpture makes a dramatic yet sophisticated statement in this refined, neutral living room; it's a clever twist on the traditional way of using classical statuary.

Opposite
Playing with proportion adds sparkle and wit to any interior: huge lightbulbs and industrial-scale clocks (top left); miniature models of iconic furniture designs (top right and bottom right); and a giant bedside lamp.

The iconic Eames lounge chair and ottoman are almost overshadowed by a monumental Anglepoise lamp. Over- and under-sized objects confound our notions of what to expect in a home, creating visual tension and surprise in equal measure.

We rarely grow out of enjoying child-sized furniture. Right, a tiny wooden chair looks even more diminutive placed next to a 'grown-up' desk.

A large toy sailing boat glides seamlessly into this rather grand hallway, adding a note of childhood reminiscence and filling an otherwise empty corner without threatening to overwhelm the space.

appeal of handling objects so much smaller and more delicate than we're used to.

By the same token, oversized pieces create an interesting dynamic in the home, confounding expectations and confusing our sense of scale. A very large piece can add a surreal Alice-in-Wonderland touch to an interior, creating strange proportions and a sense of drama. We also equate oversized furniture with comfort. We can imagine the bliss of a sofa that envelops us, of seating into which, to quote American interior designer Annie Elliott from a 2012 interview in the *New York Times*, 'you could run from the kitchen and do a swan dive'. These sorts of large soft furnishings usually work best generously sized spaces, however.

Knowing
Your ABCs

In any interior, stand-alone letters and the written word have the power to inspire, surprise and delight.

The written word is rarely displayed in the modern home, yet it's a fantastic source of quirky design and playful decoration. The presence of letters, words and numbers, such as large wooden characters, hand-painted quotations, vintage advertisements and carved dates and initials, adds humanity and depth to a space.

Typography is beautiful in itself. Fonts can be as intricate and individual as any other form of ornamentation, and different styles evoke very different moods: Times New Roman, for example (below, left), could be characterized as stoic and traditional; Gill Sans (below, right) has a chic metropolitan charm. Calligraphy, too, is a wonderful decorative resource. The ornate swirls of copperplate writing, or the rich colours of illuminated text, make sumptuous materials for pictures, wall hangings such as tapestries and silkscreens, and wallpaper.

Use letters to create visual jokes, tell a story and make people laugh. Amusing quotations and such quirky ephemera as this vintage theatre sign (right) make it easy to raise a smile.

Letters personalize a space. This child's bedroom features initials, but you can also decorate with first names and family names to put an instant stamp of ownership on your home.

We are drawn to lettering in the home for a number of reasons. Words can convey strong messages or teasing humour. We can instantly personalize a space by displaying our own initials or names. We may love the quirky charm of a retro shop sign or a railway placard, especially if they hold associations with our home town or other significant location. But also, letters and numbers can be graphic art in their own right. Their sharp lines or sinuous curves can be deeply pleasing, and we appreciate them for themselves, not just as symbols for communication. From an early age we are taught to recognize written symbols and respond to them; when they're displayed in the home we can't help but sit up and take notice.

Right, top
In this unashamedly retro-chic home, a vintage bus roll sign listing towns on a bygone route both acts as wall art and evokes a strong sense of place.

Right
A wall adorned with quotations from films ('You leave town tonight …', *Pulp Fiction*, 1994) and such twentieth-century icons as Marilyn Monroe ('I am not interested in money, I just want to be wonderful') provides a witty and powerful backdrop in this sophisticated, contemporary dining space.

Love
Lettering

Lettering offers an excellent opportunity to be both
inventive and practical in the home. From characterful
quotations to quirky labels, the written word can be both
informative and inspirational. Here are some great ways
to decorate with fonts, words and phrases.

Meaningful Quotations

If a quotation or a saying speaks to you, why not incorporate it into your decor? A beautifully hand-painted quotation, humorous phrase or family motto can inject meaning and resonance into any room, as well as being delightfully decorative.

Labels, Labels and More Labels

Take control of clutter: there's real satisfaction to be had from creating an organized, well-ordered home. Labelling storage will make your life infinitely easier, and you can be creative with your type. Options could include handwritten luggage tags, stencilled labels, labels made with a retro Dymo machine, and elegant embossed card.

Initials and Names

Few of us can resist the urge to personalize. The odd initial or monogram can look striking in an interior and can add a deeply personal touch. Salvage yards and flea markets can be heavenly hunting grounds for vintage examples, such as large pub lettering, printer's blocks, children's wooden alphabets, wrought-iron initials and delicately painted porcelain.

Framed Fonts and Calligraphy

Fonts can be beautiful. Each letter and symbol has been painstakingly designed to be pleasing both in isolation and as part of a group. Both typography (printed words) and calligraphy (handwriting) are art forms and worth celebrating in the home; a page of arresting type or lettering looks fantastic when it is framed.

Vintage
Signs

Be adventurous with traditional signage so as to create visual puns around the home. To add surprise and good-natured humour to doorways, halls and other spaces, nothing can beat railway 'Waiting Room' signs, ornate WC icons, neon writing from nightclubs, old name plaques, optician's reading charts, enamel advertising, old shop signs, antique public notices, warning signs and carved signposts.

Weird and Wonderful

There is always a set of rules behind the design and decoration of a home: a lavatory doesn't go in a kitchen; a bed's place is not in the hallway; some rooms are for public use, others are strictly private. These rules help us to make sense of our living places, and they ensure that, whichever house we find ourselves in, we can navigate and use the space without misunderstanding.

The same principle applies to decor. There's a tacit understanding that one wouldn't put a bathtub in a living room, or block a window with a bookcase. But rules are made to be broken. And that's when stimulating, characterful interiors can develop.

You can use the element of surprise to bring dynamism and personality to the home, by, for example, making visual gags and clever juxtapositions, and by using unusual materials. The measures you take should not be impractical – you need a functioning, comfortable living space – but they can be inventive.

Sometimes surprise can come from the choice of room colour. A Georgian wood-panelled room painted fluorescent green, a shocking-pink urban kitchen, a pitch-black bathroom ... exciting things can happen when magnolia paint is given a miss. Surprise can also result from a traditional object being given a makeover: a Victorian armchair covered in bold 1960s fabric, for

Opposite
This jumble of colours, patterns and eras forms an exuberant and personality-packed interior. The judicious use of a plain grey background stops the cheerful mix from descending into chaos.

Right
Animal prints, bold colours and highly decorated pieces unite to create this spirited interior. As in the photograph opposite, a plain backdrop prevents the effect from being overwhelming.

example, or a country dresser given a retro high-gloss paint finish.

Conventions of old-fashioned taste can be subverted through the application of a touch of humour. A wall-mounted moose's head made from plywood, for example (see photograph p. 153), not only makes a clever design statement but also says something about the homeowner's views on traditional hunting trophies. A marble bust contributes a formal note; the addition of a jaunty party hat transforms formal into distinctly informal. People often use retro or tacky ornaments in this way, to add a note of self-mockery to an otherwise flawless interior. Equally, if we can poke fun at ourselves in some way, such as

displaying funny photographs or spurious certificates of achievement, it never fails to lighten the mood. The downstairs WC is often a favourite candidate for this sort of fun, as its inherently base function only adds to the desired gently ironic tone.

Darker humour, too, can have a place in the home if used sparingly. As regards salvage, for example, some fascinating pieces can come from buildings or professions not usually associated with domestic interiors. Hospitals, chemists, dentist's surgeries, butcher's shops, schools and other institutions can give up treasures that work brilliantly in a modern interior; think of wooden butcher's blocks, laboratory lamps,

Opposite, top
In this dining space, both the towering pile of hardbacks and the winding, curling bookshelf act as sculpture, in an original and unexpected display of the owner's prized reads.

Opposite
Taking its cue from the garish colours of India's 'Bollywood' films, this compact kitchen is a little slice of oddball heaven.

Turning the universal male and female motifs of public WCs into pieces of wall art not only creates a visually strong display but also pokes fun at convention.

An Aladdin's cave of crazy colour schemes and keepsakes (above), this highly individual sitting room conveys the owner's passion for exotic collectibles, sumptuous fabrics and ethnic decor. More muted is this pared-down interior (left), but it, too, contains some wonderfully offbeat items, such as a chicken-wire jug, an unglazed mirror frame, and seats artfully placed under a Van Gogh-esque painting of a chair.

hospital sluice sinks and school desks. What's more, institutional and industrial pieces are often well made and robust.

Visual tricks are fun, too. By creating illusions and reflections, for example through the use of *trompe-l'œil* frescos and mirrored sash window frames, you can alter perspective and play with space. You can also add drama with unusual juxtapositions, such as a bold 1950s lamp placed next to a slender Regency chair, a heavy Victorian painting hung on a brightly coloured wall, or a rustic, chunky wool blanket thrown on to the back of a sleek Modernist sofa. The contrasts don't have to be glaringly obvious, just strong enough to create a visual tussle between two conflicting styles.

If you're lucky enough to live in a home that has inbuilt architectural surprises, such as areas of glass flooring or hidden doorways, or have the budget to renovate, these are fantastic ways to incorporate the 'wow' factor. Period properties occasionally hold hidden gems, from watercourses and wells running beneath the floorboards to secret tunnels or

Such traditional interior-design basics as padded seating and mirrors are here given a vibrant new lease of life with unconventional paintwork and patchwork fabric. Even the teapot has been transformed with a chopped-up pattern of stripes.

priest's holes, and to display and enjoy these rare treats in some way is a must. To realize that there's more than meets the eye or that a room can be viewed from a different perspective opens up a new, thrilling way of experiencing a living environment. Hidden cellars and bolt-holes, ingenious storage solutions, attic spaces and cleverly placed screens can all create a feeling of discovery and delight. And it's then, when your home becomes more than just a place to pass through unnoticed, that you know you've made somewhere really special – a truly creative, quirky and characterful home.

Directory

Who to Ask

American Institute for Conservation of Historic and Artistic Works (AIC)

Conservation website with excellent advice on the care and maintenance of heirlooms and works of art.
www.conservation-us.org

Conservation Register

The resource for finding professionally qualified conservator-restorers in the UK and Ireland. Specialists on everything from embroidery to antique clocks.
www.conservationregister.com

The Georgian Group

Advice and grants for restoration for owners of Georgian properties in Great Britain. See also the American Friends of the Georgian Group and the Irish Georgian Society.
www.georgiangroup.org.uk
www.americangeorgians.org
www.igs.ie

Guild of Master Craftsmen

UK-based register of skilled and reputable craftspeople, including traditional builders, carpenters, skilled tradespeople, specialist craftsworkers and designer-makers.
www.findacraftsman.com

Old Houses

US-based resource offering historic homes for sale or rent, suppliers and services, and old guides to house style.
www.oldhouses.com

Period Property UK

Improvement and insurance advice for period homes and listed building, and listings of period properties for sale.
www.periodproperty.co.uk

The Society for the Protection of Ancient Buildings (SPAB)

Courses for homeowners on the repair and care of old buildings. Free online information sheets on everything from timber floorboards to lime plaster.
www.spab.org.uk

Twentieth Century Society

Publications, advice, lectures and other events to support and advise owners of post-1914 buildings.
www.c20society.org.uk

The Victorian Society

Information on looking after Victorian and Edwardian houses, and online advice on everything from nineteenth-century interior decor to decorative tiles.
www.victoriansociety.org.uk

Where to Buy

ABC Home

High-end US home decor boutique with a strong sense of green issues, sustainable design and social responsibility.
www.abchome.com

Affordable Art Fairs

Contemporary affordable art fairs held worldwide, throughout the year, from Melbourne to Mexico City.
www.affordableartfair.com

Andy Thornton

Architectural antiques and interior accessories from one of largest suppliers of salvage and reclamation items in the UK – and the world.
www.andythornton.com

Anthropologie

Statement furniture, one-of-a-kind homeware and innovative gifts. Everything from retro-inspired wallpaper to quirky knobs and hooks.
www.anthropologie.eu
http://us.anthropologie.com

Antikbar

Original and reproduction vintage poster art.
www.antikbar.co.uk

Baileys Home and Garden

Homeware focusing on quirky salvage, and recycled and repurposed objects.
www.baileyshomeandgarden.com

Bloomingdales

High-quality homeware and gifts from a wide range of designers and decorators.
www.bloomingdales.com

Bromleighs

Manufacturers and suppliers of period feature sockets and switches, electrical accessories, interior and exterior lighting, and architectural hardware.
www.bromleighs.com

Cabbages and Roses

Vintage homeware and own-brand fabrics. Specialists in floral linens and toiles for light upholstery, curtains and soft furnishings.
www.cabbagesandroses.com

Degree Art

Sells, commissions and rents affordable artwork by the students and recent graduates of prestigious art establishments.
www.degreeart.com

Designers Guild

Designers Guild fabric and wallpaper, plus Royal Collection, William Yeoward and Christian Lacroix fabrics.
www.designersguild.com

Etsy

Marketplace website for vintage and home-made furniture and accessories from around the world.
www.etsy.com

Fabrics & Papers

Online one-stop shop for designer fabric and wallcoverings, including such small independents as Kate Forman, Celia Birtwell and Lewis & Wood.
www.fabricsandpapers.com

Farrow & Ball

Online advice about eco paints, historic colours and finishes, and traditional limewashes. Buy paint and paper online or find a European or US stockist.
www.farrow-ball.com

Fired Earth

High-quality, globally sourced wall and floor tiles, bathrooms, kitchens and eco-friendly paint.
www.firedearth.com

Heal's

Design classics and contemporary furniture and homeware from prominent and new designers. Strong emphasis on craftsmanship and timeless design.
www.heals.co.uk

Historic Lighting

Vintage industrial and retro lighting for use in the modern home.
www.historiclighting.co.uk

House Directory

Online sourcebook for interior and garden decoration. Lists suppliers of vintage, antique and retro homeware, and specialist services and suppliers.
www.thehousedirectory.com

Ian Mankin

Natural and organic textiles made in the UK. Best known for its collection of tickings, stripes, checks and plains.
www.ianmankin.co.uk

IKEA

Particularly good for inventive, inexpensive storage solutions: everything from laundry baskets to photo boxes.
www.ikea.com

International Antiques & Collectors Fairs

Fairs for everything for the period or modern home, from fine antique furniture to stunning vintage fabrics.
www.iacf.co.uk

Jayson Home

Ever-evolving mix of modern and one-of-a-kind vintage furniture, tableware, lighting, candles, books, pillows, textiles and more.
www.jaysonhome.com

Jim Lawrence

Craftsworker-made ironmongery, lighting, switches and sockets for period and contemporary homes. Also soft furnishings.
www.jim-lawrence.co.uk

Labour and Wait

Products from specialist makers from around the world, many of which manufacture their goods in the traditional way and to original designs.
www.labourandwait.co.uk

Liberty

Emporium noted for one-off pieces, design classics, craft innovation and high-quality furnishings.
www.liberty.co.uk

Little Greene Paint Company

Paint and luxury wallpaper based on historic designs inspired by the English Heritage archive, in colours to suit both period and contemporary interiors.
www.littlegreene.com

Live Auctioneers

Browse upcoming auctions around the world, search for particular items, and make bids online.
www.liveauctioneers.com

Made.com

Well-designed and beautifully crafted furniture, storage and lighting directly from the makers.
www.made.com

mydeco.com

European furniture and homeware from hundreds of independent, high-end boutiques and designers.
www.mydeco.com

Normann Copenhagen

Danish homeware and gifts store. Also carries children's furniture and design.
http://normann-copenhagen.com

Not on the High Street

Gifts and homeware from creative designers and small, independent manufacturers.
www.notonthehighstreet.com

Paperchase

Design-led art supplies, craft materials, gifts and stationery.
www.paperchase.co.uk

RE

Found objects, recycled treasures and cool salvage; everything from deck-chair canvas to finishing touches.
www.re-foundobjects.com

Robert Welch

Knives, cookware and utensils handmade by UK award-winning design studio. The website also links to Robert Welch USA.
www.robertwelch.com

SALVO

Gateway to worldwide suppliers of architectural salvage, antiques and reclaimed building materials.
www.salvoweb.com
www.salvo.co.uk
www.salvo.us

The Society Inc

Australia-based source of vintage treasures and old curiosities. Also runs workshops on creating beautiful interiors.
www.thesocietyinc.com.au

Wesley-Barrell

Custom-made upholstered furniture from an award-winning UK-based family business, in both classic and contemporary designs.
www.wesley-barrell.co.uk

Willow & Stone

Replica and reclaimed architectural fittings and ironmongery.
www.willowandstone.co.uk

What to Browse

Apartment Therapy

Blog exploring the underlying elements of homes and living; everything from organization to green technology, and from comfort to family life.
www.apartmenttherapy.com

Bodie and Fou

Online store and blog about modern, characterful styling for the home. Brings together high-quality European designs with chic homeware and French furniture.
www.bodieandfou.com
www.bodieandfou.blogspot.co.uk

Decor8

For all things design and decor: lots of quirky ideas, characterful homes and unusual takes on conventional interiors.
http://decor8blog.com

Design Sponge

Website and blog focusing on creating deeply personal living spaces; gives peeks into the homes of visual-art designers.
www.designsponge.com

Design Squish

US-based blog about the relationship between sustainablility, nature, home design and art.
http://blog.designsquish.com

Houzz

Vast collection of home decor images. Create an online 'scrapbook' of photos, consult the Q&As and browse products.
www.houzz.com

Katy Elliott

Online journal about New England life, decorating inspiration, and renovating a 260-year-old house in Marblehead, Massachusetts. An object lesson in how to put back the character in an old house.
www.katyelliott.com

Print & Pattern

British blog dedicated to all things patterned and printed.
http://printpattern.blogspot.co.uk

SF Girl By Bay

Quirky blog from a San Francisco-based photographer, stylist, design junkie and flea-market queen. Features shopping tips and design resources.
www.sfgirlbybay.com

The Style Files

Netherlands-based blog about home design and style. Observations and ideas about design, interiors and art with a quirky, European emphasis.
http://style-files.com

What to Read

Mark and Sally Bailey, *Handmade Home: Living with Art and Craft*, London (Ryland Peters & Small) 2011

—, *Recycled Home*, London (Ryland Peters & Small) 2007

Sally Bevan, *The Reclaimers: A Complete Guide to Salvage*, London (Hodder & Stoughton) 2005

Julia Bird, *The Naturally Scented Home*, London (Collins & Brown) 2000

Hans Blomquist, *The Natural Home*, London (Ryland Peters & Small) 2012

Ros Byam Shaw, *Farrow & Ball: Living With Colour*, London (Ryland Peters & Small) 2010

Emily Chalmers, *Modern Vintage Style*, London (Ryland Peters & Small) 2011

Sibella Court, *Etcetera: Creating Beautiful Interiors with the Things You Love*, London (Murdoch) 2010

Marianne Cusato, Leon Krier and Richard Sammons, *Get Your House Right: Architectural Elements to Use and Avoid*, New York (Sterling) and Lewes (GMC Distribution) 2011

Lili Diallo, *Details: A Stylist's Secrets to Creating Inspired Interiors*, New York (Clarkson Potter) 2010

Robin Forster and Tim Whittaker, *The Well-Worn Interior*, London (Thames & Hudson) 2003

Leslie Geddes-Brown *Books Do Furnish a Room*, London (Merrell) 2009

Geraldine James, *Creative Walls: How to Display and Enjoy Your Treasured Collections*, London (Cico Books) 2011

Judith H. Miller, *Period Details Sourcebook*, London (Mitchell Beazley) 1999

Monica Rich Kosann, *Living with What You Love*, New York (Clarkson Potter) 2010

Richard Sennett, *The Craftsman*, London (Allen Lane) 2008

Katherine Sorrell, *The Vintage/Modern Home*, London (Merrell) 2011

Judith Wilson, *Casual Living: No-fuss Style for a Comfortable Home*, London (Ryland Peters & Small) 2010

Rebecca Winward, *Happy Home*, London (Merrell) 2012

Picture Credits

Key:
b = bottom; c = centre; l = left; r = right; t = top

Victoria Harley: 7, 8, 9t, 25c, 37b, 39cr, 39l, 45, 56b, 57l, 58, 59, 71b, 72, 78t, 79, 84br, 103tr, 111tr, 157b, 160l, 168tl, 170, 171t

Photoshot/Food & Drink: 125r

Photoshot/Lived in Images/Tyson Ellis: 148bl

Photoshot/Lived in Images/Eric Hernandez: 147b

Photoshot/Lived in Images/Jessie Walker: 147t, 148br, 148t

Photoshot/Redcover/Oliver Beamish: 150t

Photoshot/Redcover/Steve Dalton: 57r, 117cr, 124t, 142l, 143

Photoshot/Redcover/Jerome Darblay: 156

Photoshot/Redcover/Serena De Sanctis: 25bl

Photoshot/Redcover/Christopher Drake: 12, 19tl, 19tr, 25tc, 39r, 50b, 55, 57cl, 80, 81t, 82t, 85b, 88, 91b, 96b, 103tl, 103b, 106b, 121t, 127t, 136r, 168b, 178b

Photoshot/Redcover/Claudia Dulak: 105

Photoshot/Redcover/Michelle Garrett: 113br, 116l, 116r

Photoshot/Redcover/David George: 4, 16, 20b, 36tr, 56t, 110, 117cl, 123, 134, 146, 153b, 159b

Photoshot/Red Cover/Douglas Gibb: 166

Photoshot/Redcover/Victoria Gomez: 116cl

Photoshot/Redcover/Grant Govier: 154

Photoshot/Redcover/Stewart Grant: 65br

Photoshot/Redcover/Ken Hayden: 9b, 46, 49, 65bl, 75b, 78b, 81b, 85t, 109, 112, 133, 140t, 177

Photoshot/Redcover/Modeste Herwig: 125l

Photoshot/Redcover/Richard Holt: 176t

Photoshot/Red Cover/Home Journal: 35, 68b, 145, 163c, 165br

Photoshot/Redcover/David Jacquot: 19br

Photoshot/Redcover/James Kerr: 97t, 100

Photoshot/Redcover/Sandra Lane: 14t, 107t, 125cr, 173r, 174, 179

Photoshot/Redcover/Nicolas Lemonnier: 180

Photoshot/Redcover/Di Lewis: 13, 17b, 33, 37t, 50t, 57cr, 63r, 74, 94, 106t, 111tl, 129r

Photoshot/Redcover/Fabio Lombrici: 71t, 161, 162c, 165tl

Photoshot/Redcover/Simon McBride: 10tr, 11, 23b, 27l, 48, 62t, 65tl, 70, 75t, 84t, 95, 101, 102, 131t, 138, 140b, 150br, 159t

Photoshot/Redcover/Katarina Malmström: 54

Photoshot/Redcover/Peter Margonelli: 38t, 43r, 65tr, 157t

Photoshot/Redcover/Paul Massey: 121b

Photoshot/Redcover/Anastassios Mentis: 34t, 77tl, 129l, 135, 139, 181t

Photoshot/Redcover/James Mitchell: 34b, 61, 117l

Photoshot/Redcover/Laura Moss: 10tl, 31, 83, 95, 144

Photoshot/Redcover/Sophie Munro: 24t, 41, 84bl, 89t, 150bl, 163r

Photoshot/Redcover/Flore Palix/Oredia: 25tl, 25tr, 30, 51, 90, 93, 113bl, 118l, 136l, 158, 162l, 163l

Photoshot/Redcover/David Prince: 24b, 77tr, 82b, 111b, 117r

Photoshot/Redcover/Quickimage/Emilio Rodriguez: 59

Photoshot/Redcover/Ed Reeve: 39cl

Photoshot/Redcover/Felipe Scheffel: 108

Photoshot/Redcover/Grant Scott: 165bl, 167t, 167b

Photoshot/Redcover/Keith Scott Morton: jacket front, 21

Photoshot/Redcover/Evan Sklar: 25br, 67, 97b, 99, 118r, 125cl, 142r, 165tr

Photoshot/Redcover/Michal Skorupski: 171b

Photoshot/Redcover/Patrick Spence: 15, 28, 29

Photoshot/Redcover/Sue Stubbs: 14b, 113tr

Photoshot/Redcover/Jonathan Thomas: 40, 42, 43l, 119, 120, 122b

Photoshot/Redcover/Scott Van Dyke: 173l

Photoshot/Redcover/Deborah Whitlaw-Llewellyn: 27r, 149, 168tr

Photoshot/Redcover/Henry Wilson: 10b, 17t, 22br, 23t, 36tl, 36b, 38b, 47b, 52t, 52b, 60, 62b, 63l, 73, 77bl, 91t, 96t, 98, 104, 113tl, 115t, 128, 130, 132t, 153t, 155, 162r, 164, 175, 176b

Photoshot/Redcover/Andrew Wood: 20t, 22t, 22bl, 26, 32, 77br, 86, 107b, 114, 115b, 116cr, 127b, 131b, 132b, 160r, 169, 178t

Photoshot/Redcover/Mel Yates: 30, 47t, 68t, 69, 89b, 137

Photoshot/Redcover/Viv Yeo: 122t

Photoshot/Redcover/Mark York: 181b

Photoshot/Redcover/Lukasz Zandecki: 124b

The publisher has made every effort to trace and contact copyright holders of the material reproduced in this book. It will be happy to correct in subsequent editions any errors or omissions that are brought to its attention.

Acknowledgements

This book is dedicated to baby Emma,
our new little character.

Many thanks to everyone who helped to create *A Home of Your Own*, a book I've been wanting to write for years. Thanks to Claire Chandler and Hugh Merrell for seeing that the idea had potential, for having faith in it and for putting their energy into the project. Thanks also to Alex Coco for his wonderful design eye, Marion Moisy for her razor-sharp editorial skills, Nick Wheldon for spot-on picture research, and Victoria Harley, once again, for her cracking photography.

Index

First published 2013 by
Merrell Publishers, London and New York

Merrell Publishers Limited
81 Southwark Street
London SE1 0HX

merrellpublishers.com

British Library Cataloguing in Publication Data.
A catalogue record for this book is available from
the British Library.

ISBN 978-1-8589-4594-1

Produced by Merrell Publishers Limited
Designed by Alexandre Coco
Project-managed by Marion Moisy
Indexed by Hilary Bird

Printed and bound in China

Jacket front: see page 21
Jacket back (clockwise from
top left): see pages 171, 98,
145, 99